First World War
Poems from the Front

Paul O'Prey is Vice-Chancellor of the University of Roehampton, London, and a Professor of Modern Literature. After studying at Oxford in the 1970s, he lived with and worked for Robert Graves, whose poems, letters and essays he has edited.

First World War Poems from the Front

Edited by
PAUL O'PREY

First published in 2014 by IWM,
Lambeth Road, London SE1 6HZ
iwm.org.uk

ISBN 978-1-904897-88-0

A catalogue record for this book is available
from the British Library.
Designed by James Alexander www.jadedesign.co.uk
Printed by Graphicom SrL

All images © IWM unless otherwise stated.
Cover image © Shutterstock.com

Every effort has been made to contact all copyright
holders. The publishers will be glad to make good
in future editions any error or omissions brought to
their attention.

1 3 5 7 9 10 8 6 4 2

In memory of Captain Robert Graves,
Royal Welch Fusiliers, who first made me realise
the power of these poems.

Contents

Introduction

Perhaps the first, rather paradoxical, thing to say about war poetry, is that no matter how much we might admire it, or how deeply it might affect us, we must surely wish it had not been written. The price of becoming a war poet was intolerably high. At the least, it meant physical or mental trauma; for many, it meant violent death. It is hard to exaggerate the horror to which these young poets bore witness.

A century on, there is still no consensus on whether the First World War was justified or 'necessary'. It was a particularly brutal conflict. Over nine million people died in action, with millions more permanently damaged by injury, mental breakdown, or grief for the death of those they loved. The world had little to show in return for so much loss. The war did not stabilise global politics, but was soon followed by a Second World War. For many people after 1918, the world seemed a darker, less hopeful, less decent place.

This of course is a perspective of the war based on one hundred years of hindsight, and almost seventy years of peace in Britain. Things looked different in the summer of 1914. Although not everyone was enthusiastic about the coming war, it did have a great deal of popular support, and during the course of the conflict many people, including many poets, continued to believe in the cause for which they were fighting.

The modern popularity of certain poets, especially Siegfried Sassoon and Wilfred Owen, has sometimes led to a view that all war poetry is anti-war poetry. Their savage, bitter poems, deliberately written to shock and challenge, have gripped our imagination with a vivid picture of innocent young men broken by meaningless violence, victims of an incompetent, misguided state. Any wider reading of the poetry written at the front, however, reveals that other poets held other views, and some shifted their position as the war progressed.

Overall, the attitude to the war expressed in war poetry is wide-ranging, complex and frequently ambiguous. In 'This is no case of petty right or wrong', Edward Thomas feels no specific hate of Germans, and refuses to 'grow hot /With love of Englishmen, to please newspapers'. Instead he describes a patriotism that seems more existential than political. Robert von Ranke Graves, as he was then known, volunteered at the outbreak of war, keen to fight for 'England's cause', even though he loved his German mother deeply and was proud of his distinguished German forebears. He became disillusioned by the official handling of the war, but remained driven by a fierce loyalty to the men with whom he served, and the values of his regiment. Geoffrey Studdert Kennedy preached a Christian message of love and peace to troops at the front, but he was not a pacifist. For all they were against the war, both Sassoon and Owen were awarded the Military Cross for exceptional leadership and bravery in battle. The incident which led to Owen's decoration was described vividly in the official citation: 'He personally manipulated a captured enemy M.G. [machine gun] from an isolated position and inflicted considerable losses on the enemy.'

The poets included in this anthology, all of whom saw active service, represent a broad range of perspectives, though some common themes are striking. There is, for example, no hatred of the enemy, rather a deep bond with fellow combatants, as well as a wider compassion for humanity. This compassion is extended, in the case of Vera Brittain, to include the wounded enemy soldiers she nurses in the prisoner ward. As the foundations of their world are shaken, the transcending values of love, friendship, communion with the natural world, are thrown into sharp focus, as the poets yearn for peace and lament lost innocence and goodness. These are poems that come close to Robert Frost's desire for poetry to provide 'a clarification of life […] a momentary stay against confusion'.

In seeking to write about the war, poets drew on a variety of poetic styles and techniques, ranging from the Kiplingesque rhymes of Geoffrey Studdert Kennedy to the dislocated modernism of David Jones. Most of the poets, however, can be seen pushing traditional boundaries to some extent or other, reaching for new effects and a new diction to describe an unprecedented horror, which the old forms struggled to contain. In doing so, they play their part in the transformation of English poetry that took place in the early twentieth century.

This anthology brings together fifteen poets who were in uniform and who saw active service on the front line, whether as a soldier fighting the enemy, as a nurse or medical orderly looking after the wounded, or in the case of Studdert Kennedy, as a military chaplain giving moral support in any way he could. Some are officers, while others, like Isaac Rosenberg and Ivor Gurney, served in the ranks, where conditions were particularly harsh. Three of the poets are women, and though they were not allowed to take part in the fighting, they served in other ways. As front line nurses, Vera Brittain and Mary Borden were tested to the limit of physical and emotional endurance, ministering to an overwhelming flow of wounded and dying men, with no access to modern treatments for pain or infection. Some of the poems were scribbled down in the very heat of battle, or in field hospitals, sometimes with no chance either then or later to revise and edit them. Others, by poets who survived the war, like Edmund Blunden and Ivor Gurney, were written in retrospect, with time to reflect on what had been seen and done. What brings these poets together is that they all wrote with the authority that comes from direct experience, and with the commitment to truthful witness that guarantees the authenticity of their work.

The war saw a tremendous flourishing of poetry on a scale not seen before or since. Thousands of people took to writing poetry, millions took to reading it. Much of this poetry has not endured, and many of the poets who dominated early anthologies are now forgotten. These same anthologies gave little or no space to some of the poets we value most today, like Wilfred Owen, Isaac Rosenberg, Edward Thomas and Ivor Gurney. Tastes change, attitudes change, and it can take time for a poetic voice to be heard above the crowd, especially when the subject is so emotionally explosive.

When WB Yeats compiled the influential *Oxford Book of Modern Verse* in 1936, he excluded war poetry and was particularly disparaging about Owen. He has not been alone in finding war poetry to be lacking in artistic skill, and it has to be said that much of it is the early work of young and technically immature poets. In more normal circumstances, such early work is often dropped from a poet's lifetime collection. That said, modern audiences have become more accustomed to admiring art that seems incomplete or impressionistic, even crudely executed, if it speaks in a voice that is authentic, truthful and direct.

It is for this reason I have included, in a few instances, what are clearly only drafts or fragments of poems. Rupert Brooke's account of wandering about the deck of his ship at night, watching the men playing cards, was written just before his death and gives a glimpse of how he might have gone on to write about the war, had he survived. Charles Sorley was still working on the poem found in his kit-bag when he was killed. Three of Mary Borden's poems exist only as handwritten drafts and have not been published in book form until now. They are deeply passionate, spontaneous outbursts that paint a vivid picture of her life running a field hospital. Also included is 'November 11th', an early draft of an intensely bitter 'street ballad' by Graves, taken from a 1918 letter to Edward Marsh, editor of the Georgian Poetry anthologies. It appears here for the first time as a poem in its own right. Graves's contempt for the crowds celebrating the Armistice was so unrestrained that he was persuaded not to publish it. He finally released a much toned-down version in 1969, saying that it had been 'unprintable' until then.

The war poets are predominantly young men and women, finding themselves at the extreme edge of human experience, overwhelmed with feelings and emotions we can barely imagine, seeking to describe a territory in which words seem inadequate. If they were sitting between battles, in muddy dugouts and trenches, or in overcrowded hospital wards, penning highly-polished, elegantly-turned sonnets, we might well regard them with some suspicion. This is why modern readers tend to distrust Rupert Brooke, though his famous sonnet sequence encapsulated the spirit of those heady days at the start of war, and even Yeats admired them. At first, many poets took Brooke as their model in writing about the war, though they tended to adjust their position after first-hand experience of the trenches, which Brooke himself did not live long enough to see. Charles Sorley was, however, unconvinced by Brooke's authenticity from the start, writing home to say: 'He is far too obsessed with his own sacrifice [...] he has clothed his attitude in fine words: but he has taken the sentimental attitude'.

Sentimentalism, fine words, false attitudes, have not stood the test of time. There is, on the other hand, a rawness, energy, and urgent truthfulness about the poetry written by Owen, Sorley, Gurney, Rosenberg, Borden and others, which demands our attention. Their burningly insistent messages, from the very limit of endurable human experience, are sent without time to reflect or polish words and ideas. It is this urgency and this authenticity – the force of their anger, fear, despair, love and confusion – which resonates with a modern audience. Their relative lack of experience as poets is itself expressive of the endeavour. Owen famously said that for him the poetry is in the pity. For his readers the poetry is also in the innocence.

Owen knew that his 'elegies' offered little in the way of consolation to his own generation. All a poet in his situation could do, he said, was to tell the truth, and to warn: if his poems held any consolation, it might only be for future generations. In that, too, he was right.

Paul O'Prey

Rupert Brooke
1887 – 1915

Rupert Brooke grew up in Rugby, Warwickshire. His father was a master at Rugby School, where Brooke himself was a pupil. He studied Classics at Cambridge and in 1913 won a fellowship at King's College. With Edward Marsh, he established the series of Georgian Poetry anthologies which, after their first appearance in 1912, did much to popularise contemporary poetry. In 1913 he travelled to Canada, the USA and Tahiti.

At the outbreak of war he took a commission with the Royal Naval Division, saying: 'If Armageddon is *on*, I suppose one should be there'. In October 1914 he arrived in Belgium to see thousands of refugees fleeing Antwerp after it had been taken by German forces. Being 'a witness to one of the greatest crimes of history' strengthened his resolve about the war. In February 1915 he sailed to Gallipoli with the Hood Battalion. Before seeing action, he died of blood poisoning, probably from an infected mosquito bite, on a French hospital ship off the Greek island of Skyros.

Brooke's war sonnets captured a prevailing spirit of patriotic zeal. They were instantly popular, deeply admired and widely imitated. At his death (on St George's Day, 1915), Brooke came to embody a national myth of golden youth and innocence sacrificing itself for love of a noble country. He died before he himself had the chance to question this view of the war, and his own role in it.

The Dead

These hearts were woven of human joys and cares,
   Washed marvellously with sorrow, swift to mirth.
The years had given them kindness. Dawn was theirs,
   And sunset, and the colours of the earth.
These had seen movement, and heard music; known
   Slumber and waking; loved; gone proudly friended;
Felt the quick stir of wonder; sat alone;
   Touched flowers and furs and cheeks. All this is ended.

There are waters blown by changing winds to laughter
And lit by the rich skies, all day. And after,
   Frost, with a gesture, stays the waves that dance
And wandering loveliness. He leaves a white
   Unbroken glory, a gathered radiance,
A width, a shining peace, under the night.

The Soldier

If I should die, think only this of me:
   That there's some corner of a foreign field
That is for ever England. There shall be
   In that rich earth a richer dust concealed;
A dust whom England bore, shaped, made aware,
   Gave, once, her flowers to love, her ways to roam,
A body of England's, breathing English air,
   Washed by the rivers, blest by suns of home.

And think, this heart, all evil shed away,
   A pulse in the eternal mind, no less
     Gives somewhere back the thoughts by England given;
Her sights and sounds; dreams happy as her day;
   And laughter, learnt of friends; and gentleness,
     In hearts at peace, under an English heaven.

I strayed about the deck

I strayed about the deck, an hour, to-night
Under a cloudy moonless sky; and peeped
In at the windows, watched my friends at table,
Or playing cards, or standing in the doorway,
Or coming out into the darkness. Still
No one could see me.

        I would have thought of them
– Heedless, within a week of battle – in pity,
Pride in their strength and in the weight and firmness
And link'd beauty of bodies, and pity that
This gay machine of splendour 'ld soon be broken,
Thought little of, pashed, scattered...

        Only, always,
I could but see them – against the lamplight – pass
Like coloured shadows, thinner than filmy glass,
Slight bubbles, fainter than the wave's faint light,
That broke to phosphorus out in the night,
Perishing things and strange ghosts – soon to die
To other ghosts – this one, or that, or I.

Charles Sorley
1895 – 1915

Charles Hamilton Sorley grew up in Cambridge, where his father was Professor of Moral Philosophy. In early 1914, before going to Oxford, Sorley set off on an extended visit to Germany, studying Literature and Philosophy at the University of Jena. When war broke out in August he headed home. On the way he was arrested and held briefly in Trier. Immediately on his return to Britain, the nineteen-year-old Sorley enlisted, taking a commission with the Suffolk Regiment. His philosophical maturity and high regard for German culture meant he did not share in the general wave of enthusiasm for the coming battle, or feel a jingoistic hatred of the enemy. This made him an unusual recruit in 1914. Just before embarking for France he wrote to his mother: 'I do wish that people would not deceive themselves by talk of a just war. There is no such thing [...] what we are doing is casting out Satan by Satan.'

In September 1915 Sorley's battalion took part in the Loos offensive. By now a Captain, he was shot by a sniper on 13 October, while inspecting trench defences. A pencil draft of the poem, 'When you see millions of the mouthless dead', was found in his kit-bag. Sorley did not have the time to polish his work or prepare his poems for publication. They appeared for the first time after his death, in 1916.

All the hills and vales along

All the hills and vales along
Earth is bursting into song,
And the singers are the chaps
Who are going to die perhaps.
    O sing, marching men,
    Till the valleys ring again.
    Give your gladness to earth's keeping,
    So be glad, when you are sleeping.

Cast away regret and rue,
Think what you are marching to.
Little live, great pass.
Jesus Christ and Barabbas
Were found the same day.
This died, that went his way.
    So sing with joyful breath.
    For why, you are going to death.
    Teeming earth will surely store
    All the gladness that you pour.

Earth that never doubts nor fears,
Earth that knows of death, not tears,
Earth that bore with joyful ease
Hemlock for Socrates,
Earth that blossomed and was glad
'Neath the cross that Christ had,
Shall rejoice and blossom too
When the bullet reaches you.
    Wherefore, men marching
    On the road to death, sing!
    Pour your gladness on earth's head,
    So be merry so be dead.

From the hills and valleys earth
Shouts back the sound of mirth,
Tramp of feet and lilt of song
Ringing all the road along
All the music of their going,
Ringing swinging glad song-throwing,
Earth will echo still, when foot
Lies numb and voice mute.
    On marching men, on
    To the gates of death with song.
    Sow your gladness for earth's reaping,
    So you may be glad, though sleeping.
    Strew your gladness on earth's bed,
    So be merry, so be dead.

To Germany

You are blind like us. Your hurt no man designed,
And no man claimed the conquest of your land.
But gropers both through fields of thought confined
We stumble and we do not understand.
You only saw your future bigly planned,
And we, the tapering paths of our own mind,
And in each other's dearest ways we stand,
And hiss and hate. And the blind fight the blind.

When it is peace, then we may view again
With new-won eyes each other's truer form
And wonder. Grown more loving-kind and warm
We'll grasp firm hands and laugh at the old pain,
When it is peace. But until peace, the storm
The darkness and the thunder and the rain.

Two Sonnets

I

Saints have adored the lofty soul of you.
Poets have whitened at your high renown.
We stand among the many millions who
Do hourly wait to pass your pathway down.
You, so familiar, once were strange: we tried
To live as of your presence unaware.
But now in every road on every side
We see your straight and steadfast signpost there.

I think it like that signpost in my land,
Hoary and tall, which pointed me to go
Upward, into the hills, on the right hand,
Where the mists swim and the winds shriek and blow,
A homeless land and friendless, but a land
I did not know and that I wished to know.

II

Such, such is Death: no triumph: no defeat:
Only an empty pail, a slate rubbed clean,
A merciful putting away of what has been.

And this we know: Death is not Life effete,
Life crushed, the broken pail. We who have seen
So marvellous things know well the end not yet.

Victor and vanquished are a-one in death:
Coward and brave: friend, foe. Ghosts do not say
'Come, what was your record when you drew breath?'
But a big blot has hid each yesterday
So poor, so manifestly incomplete.
And your bright Promise, withered long and sped,
Is touched, stirs, rises, opens and grows sweet
And blossoms and is you, when you are dead.

When you see millions of the mouthless dead

When you see millions of the mouthless dead
Across your dreams in pale battalions go,
Say not soft things as other men have said,
That you'll remember. For you need not so.
Give them not praise. For, deaf, how should they know
It is not curses heaped on each gashed head?
Nor tears. Their blind eyes see not your tears flow.
Nor honour. It is easy to be dead.
Say only this, 'They are dead.' Then add thereto,
'Yet many a better one has died before.'
Then, scanning all the o'ercrowded mass, should you
Perceive one face that you loved heretofore,
It is a spook. None wears the face you knew.
Great death has made all his for evermore.

Robert Graves
1895 – 1985

Robert Graves grew up in Wimbledon and volunteered immediately on the outbreak of war. He had just finished school and was waiting to take up a place to study Classics at Oxford.

He served in the Royal Welch Fusiliers, rose to the rank of Captain, and was so severely wounded at the Somme that he was left for dead. Graves was one of the first soldier-poets to write in a more realistic way about his experience of the trenches. Sassoon was a fellow officer in the same regiment, and they became close friends ('Two Fusiliers'). They later argued, especially over Graves's account of the war in *Goodbye To All That* (1929). Graves suffered from neurasthenia ('shell shock') for many years after the war: 'My disabilities were many: I could not use a telephone, I felt sick every time I travelled by train, and to see more than two new people in a single day prevented me from sleeping.' He went on to become one of the leading poets of his generation, and is particularly regarded as a love poet.

Graves wrote historical novels, including *I, Claudius*, as well as two ground-breaking books on mythology, *The White Goddess* and *The Greek Myths*. He lived in Mallorca for most of his life, disillusioned with post-war England, to which he bid a bitter 'goodbye' in 1929.

A Dead Boche

To you who'd read my songs of War
   And only hear of blood and fame,
I'll say (you've heard it said before)
   'War's Hell!' and if you doubt the same,
To-day I found in Mametz Wood
A certain cure for lust of blood:

Where, propped against a shattered trunk,
   In a great mess of things unclean,
Sat a dead Boche; he scowled and stunk
   With clothes and face a sodden green,
Big-bellied, spectacled, crop-haired,
Dribbling black blood from nose and beard.

Two Fusiliers

And have we done with War at last?
Well, we've been lucky devils both,
And there's no need of pledge or oath
To bind our lovely friendship fast,
By firmer stuff
Close bound enough.

By wire and wood and stake we're bound,
By Fricourt and by Festubert,
By whipping rain, by the sun's glare,
By all the misery and loud sound,
By a Spring day,
By Picard clay.

Show me the two so closely bound
As we, by the wet bond of blood,
By friendship blossoming from mud,
By Death: we faced him, and we found
Beauty in Death,
In dead men, breath.

The Legion

'Is that the Three-and-Twentieth, Strabo mine,
Marching below, and we still gulping wine?'
From the sad magic of his fragrant cup
The red-faced old centurion started up,
Cursed, battered on the table. 'No,' he said,
'Not that! The Three-and-Twentieth Legion's dead,
Dead in the first year of this damned campaign –
The Legion's dead, dead, and won't rise again.
Pity? Rome pities her brave lads that die,
But we need pity also, you and I,
Whom Gallic spear and Belgian arrow miss,
Who live to see the Legion come to this:
Unsoldierlike, slovenly, bent on loot,
Grumblers, diseased, unskilled to thrust or shoot.
O brown cheek, muscled shoulder, sturdy thigh!
Where are they now? God! watch it straggle by,
The sullen pack of ragged, ugly swine!
Is that the Legion, Gracchus? Quick, the wine!'
'Strabo,' said Gracchus, 'you are strange to-night.
The Legion is the Legion, it's all right.
If these new men are slovenly, in your thinking,
Hell take it! you'll not better them by drinking.
They all try, Strabo; trust their hearts and hands.
The Legion is the Legion while Rome stands,
And these same men before the autumn's fall
Shall bang old Vercingetorix out of Gaul.'

November 11th

Why are they cheering and shouting
  What's all the scurry of feet
With little boys banging on kettle and can
  Wild laughter of girls in the street?

O those are the froth of the city
  The thoughtless and ignorant scum
Who hang out the bunting when war is let loose
  And for victory bang on a drum

But the boys who were killed in the battle
  Who fought with no rage and no rant
Are peacefully sleeping on pallets of mud
  Low down with the worm and the ant

Draft poem from a letter to Edward Marsh, November 1918.

The Last Day of Leave (1916)

We five looked out over the moor
At rough hills blurred with haze, and a still sea:
Our tragic day, bountiful from the first.

We would spend it by the lily lake
(High in a fold beyond the farthest ridge),
Following the cart-track till it faded out.

The time of berries and bell-heather;
Yet all that morning nobody went by
But shepherds and one old man carting turfs.

We were in love: he with her, she with him,
And I, the youngest one, the odd man out,
As deep in love with a yet nameless muse.

No cloud; larks and heath-butterflies,
And herons undisturbed fishing the streams;
A slow cool breeze that hardly stirred the grass.

When we hurried down the rocky slope,
A flock of ewes galloping off in terror,
There shone the waterlilies, yellow and white.

Deep water and a shelving bank.
Off went our clothes and in we went, all five,
Diving like trout between the lily groves.

The basket had been nobly filled:
Wine and fresh rolls, chicken and pineapple –
Our braggadocio under threat of war.

The fire on which we boiled our kettle
We fed with ling and rotten blackthorn root;
And the coffee tasted memorably of peat.

Two of us might stray off together
But never less than three kept by the fire,
Focus of our uncertain destinies.

We spoke little, our minds in tune –
A sigh or laugh would settle any theme;
The sun so hot it made the rocks quiver.

But when it rolled down level with us,
Four pairs of eyes sought mine as if appealing
For a blind-fate-aversive afterword:–

'Do you remember the lily lake?
We were all there, all five of us in love,
Not one yet killed, widowed or broken-hearted.'

The Haunted House

'Come, surly fellow, come: a song!'
    What, fools? Sing to you?
Choose from the clouded tales of wrong
    And terror I bring to you:

Of a night so torn with cries,
    Honest men sleeping
Start awake with rabid eyes,
    Bone-chilled, flesh creeping,

Of spirits in the web-hung room
    Up above the stable,
Groans, knockings in the gloom,
    The dancing table,

Of demons in the dry well
    That cheep and mutter,
Clanging of an unseen bell,
    Blood choking the gutter,

Of lust frightful, past belief,
    Lurking unforgotten,
Unrestrainable endless grief
    In breasts long rotten.

A song? What laughter or what song
    Can this house remember?
Do flowers and butterflies belong
    To a blind December?

Sergeant-Major Money

It wasn't our battalion, but we lay alongside it,
    So the story is as true as the telling is frank.
They hadn't one Line-officer left, after Arras,
    Except a batty major and the Colonel, who drank.

'B' Company Commander was fresh from the Depôt,
    An expert on gas drill, otherwise a dud;
So Sergeant-Major Money carried on, as instructed,
    And that's where the swaddies began to sweat blood.

His Old Army humour was so well-spiced and hearty
    That one poor sod shot himself, and one lost his wits;
But discipline's maintained, and back in rest-billets
    The Colonel congratulates 'B' Company on their kits.

The subalterns went easy, as was only natural
    With a terror like Money driving the machine,
Till finally two Welshmen, butties from the Rhondda,
    Bayoneted their bugbear in a field-canteen.

Well, we couldn't blame the officers, they relied on Money;
    We couldn't blame the pitboys, their courage was grand;
Or, least of all, blame Money, an old stiff surviving
    In a New (bloody) Army he couldn't understand.

The Cuirassiers of the Frontier

Goths, Vandals, Huns, Isaurian mountaineers,
Made Roman by our Roman sacrament,
We can know little (as we care little)
Of the Metropolis: her candled churches,
Her white-gowned pederastic senators,
The cut-throat factions of her Hippodrome,
The eunuchs of her draped saloons.

Here is the frontier, here our camp and place –
Beans for the pot, fodder for horses,
And Roman arms. Enough. He who among us
At full gallop, the bowstring to his ear,
Lets drive his heavy arrows, to sink
Stinging through Persian corslets damascened,
Then follows with the lance – he has our love.

The Christ bade Holy Peter sheathe his sword,
Being outnumbered by the Temple guard.
And this was prudence, the cause not yet lost
While Peter might persuade the crowd to rescue.
Peter renegued, breaking his sacrament.
With us the penalty is death by stoning,
Not to be made a bishop.

In Peter's Church there is no faith nor truth,
Nor justice anywhere in palace or court.
That we continue watchful on the rampart
Concerns no priest. A gaping silken dragon,
Puffed by the wind, suffices us for God.
We, not the City, are the Empire's soul:
A rotten tree lives only in its rind.

Recalling War

Entrance and exit wounds are silvered clean,
The track aches only when the rain reminds.
The one-legged man forgets his leg of wood,
The one-armed man his jointed wooden arm.
The blinded man sees with his ears and hands
As much or more than once with both his eyes.
Their war was fought these twenty years ago
And now assumes the nature-look of time,
As when the morning traveller turns and views
His wild night-stumbling carved into a hill.

What, then, was war? No mere discord of flags
But an infection of the common sky
That sagged ominously upon the earth
Even when the season was the airiest May.
Down pressed the sky, and we, oppressed, thrust out
Boastful tongue, clenched fist and valiant yard.
Natural infirmities were out of mode,
For Death was young again: patron alone
Of healthy dying, premature fate-spasm.

Fear made fine bed-fellows. Sick with delight
At life's discovered transitoriness,
Our youth became all-flesh and waived the mind.
Never was such antiqueness of romance,
Such tasty honey oozing from the heart.
And old importances came swimming back –
Wine, meat, log-fires, a roof over the head,
A weapon at the thigh, surgeons at call.

Even there was a use again for God –
A word of rage in lack of meat, wine, fire,
In ache of wounds beyond all surgeoning.

War was return of earth to ugly earth,
War was foundering of sublimities,
Extinction of each happy art and faith
By which the world had still kept head in air.
Protesting logic or protesting love,
Until the unendurable moment struck –
The inward scream, the duty to run mad.

And we recall the merry ways of guns –
Nibbling the walls of factory and church
Like a child, piecrust; felling groves of trees
Like a child, dandelions with a switch!
Machine-guns rattle toy-like from a hill,
Down in a row the brave tin-soldiers fall:
A sight to be recalled in elder days
When learnedly the future we devote
To yet more boastful visions of despair.

The Oldest Soldier

The sun shines warm on seven old soldiers
    Paraded in a row,
Perched like starlings on the railings –
    Give them plug-tobacco!

They'll croon you the Oldest-Soldier Song:
    Of Harry who took a holiday
From the sweat of ever thinking for himself
    Or going his own bloody way.

It was arms-drill, guard and kit-inspection,
    Like dreams of a long train-journey,
And the barrack-bed that Harry dossed on
    Went rockabye, rockabye, rockabye.

Harry kept his rifle and brasses clean,
    But Jesus Christ, what a liar!
He won the Military Medal
    For his coolness under fire.

He was never the last on parade
    Nor the first to volunteer,
And when Harry rose to be storeman
    He seldom had to pay for his beer.

Twenty-one years, and out Harry came
    To be odd-job man, or janitor,
Or commissionaire at a picture-house,
    Or, some say, bully to a whore.

But his King and Country calling Harry,
    He reported again at the Depôt,
To perch on this railing like a starling,
    The oldest soldier of the row.

Siegfried Sassoon

1886 – 1967

Sassoon had a privileged childhood in Kent, where he developed a lifelong passion for poetry and for sport, especially cricket and hunting. He studied briefly at Cambridge and in August 1914 volunteered as a trooper in the Sussex Yeomanry.

The following year he was commissioned into the Royal Welch Fusiliers. Sassoon proved an exceptionally brave and sometimes reckless officer, earning himself the nickname 'Mad Jack'. He was awarded the Military Cross for gallantry in action. He was wounded in April 1917 and sent back to Britain to recover. Disillusioned by the war, and under the influence of Bertrand Russell and other intellectual pacifists, he publicly refused to continue in his military duties. The reason, he announced in a statement read out in Parliament, was that 'the war upon which I entered as a war of defence and liberation, has now become a war of aggression and conquest'.

Unknown to Sassoon, Robert Graves intervened with senior officers to have him diagnosed as having a 'mental breakdown' due to shell shock, to save him from facing a court martial – an action which was to sour their friendship. Sassoon was sent for treatment to Craiglockhart Hospital, where he became friends with fellow patient Wilfred Owen. He later returned to front line service. After the war he devoted himself to writing poetry and a series of celebrated memoirs, including *Memoirs of an Infantry Officer* (1930).

'They'

The Bishop tells us: 'When the boys come back
They will not be the same; for they'll have fought
In a just cause: they lead the last attack
On Anti-Christ; their comrades' blood has bought
New right to breed an honourable race,
They have challenged Death and dared him face to face.'

'We're none of us the same!' the boys reply.
'For George lost both his legs; and Bill's stone blind;
Poor Jim's shot through the lungs and like to die;
And Bert's gone syphilitic: you'll not find
A chap who's served that hasn't found *some* change.'
And the Bishop said: 'The ways of God are strange!'

The Hero

'Jack fell as he'd have wished,' the Mother said,
And folded up the letter that she'd read.
'The Colonel writes so nicely.' Something broke
In the tired voice that quavered to a choke.
She half looked up. 'We mothers are so proud
Of our dead soldiers.' Then her face was bowed.

Quietly the Brother Officer went out.
He'd told the poor old dear some gallant lies
That she would nourish all her days, no doubt.
For while he coughed and mumbled, her weak eyes
Had shone with gentle triumph, brimmed with joy,
Because he'd been so brave, her glorious boy.

He thought how 'Jack', cold-footed, useless swine,
Had panicked down the trench that night the mine
Went up at Wicked Corner; how he'd tried
To get sent home, and how, at last, he died,
Blown to small bits. And no one seemed to care
Except that lonely woman with white hair.

Counter-Attack

We'd gained our first objective hours before
While dawn broke like a face with blinking eyes,
Pallid, unshaved and thirsty, blind with smoke.
Things seemed all right at first. We held their line,
With bombers posted, Lewis guns well placed,
And clink of shovels deepening the shallow trench.
   The place was rotten with dead; green clumsy legs
   High-booted, sprawled and grovelled along the saps
   And trunks, face downward, in the sucking mud,
   Wallowed like trodden sand-bags loosely filled;
   And naked sodden buttocks, mats of hair,
   Bulged, clotted heads slept in the plastering slime.
   And then the rain began, – the jolly old rain!

A yawning soldier knelt against the bank,
Staring across the morning blear with fog;
He wondered when the Allemands would get busy;
And then, of course, they started with five-nines
Traversing, sure as fate, and never a dud.
Mute in the clamour of shells he watched them burst
Spouting dark earth and wire with gusts from hell,

While posturing giants dissolved in drifts of smoke.
He crouched and flinched, dizzy with galloping fear,
Sick for escape, – loathing the strangled horror
And butchered, frantic gestures of the dead.

An officer came blundering down the trench:
'Stand-to and man the fire-step!' On he went...
Gasping and bawling, 'Fire-step... counter-attack!'
    Then the haze lifted. Bombing on the right
    Down the old sap: machine-guns on the left;
    And stumbling figures looming out in front.
    'O Christ, they're coming at us!' Bullets spat,
And he remembered his rifle... rapid fire...
And started blazing wildly... then a bang
Crumpled and spun him sideways, knocked him out
To grunt and wriggle: none heeded him; he choked
And fought the flapping veils of smothering gloom,
Lost in a blurred confusion of yells and groans...
Down, and down, and down, he sank and drowned,
Bleeding to death. The counter-attack had failed.

The Rear Guard
(Hindenburg Line, April 1917)

Groping along the tunnel, step by step,
He winked his prying torch with patching glare
From side to side, and sniffed the unwholesome air.

Tins, boxes, bottles, shapes too vague to know;
A mirror smashed, the mattress from a bed;
And he, exploring fifty feet below
The rosy gloom of battle overhead.

Tripping, he grabbed the wall; saw someone lie
Humped at his feet, half-hidden by a rug,
And stooped to give the sleeper's arm a tug.
'I'm looking for headquarters.' No reply.
'God blast your neck!' (For days he'd had no sleep,)
'Get up and guide me through this stinking place.'

Savage, he kicked a soft, unanswering heap,
And flashed his beam across the livid face
Terribly glaring up, whose eyes yet wore
Agony dying hard ten days before;
And fists of fingers clutched a blackening wound.

Alone he staggered on until he found
Dawn's ghost that filtered down a shafted stair
To the dazed, muttering creatures underground
Who hear the boom of shells in muffled sound.
At last, with sweat of horror in his hair,
He climbed through darkness to the twilight air,
Unloading hell behind him step by step.

Base Details

If I were fierce, and bald, and short of breath,
    I'd live with scarlet Majors at the Base,
And speed glum heroes up the line to death.
    You'd see me with my puffy petulant face,
Guzzling and gulping in the best hotel,
    Reading the Roll of Honour. 'Poor young chap,'
I'd say – 'I used to know his father well;
    Yes, we've lost heavily in this last scrap.'
And when the war is done and youth stone dead,
I'd toddle safely home and die – in bed.

The General

'Good-morning; good-morning!' the General said
When we met him last week on our way to the line.
Now the soldiers he smiled at are most of 'em dead,
And we're cursing his staff for incompetent swine.
'He's a cheery old card,' grunted Harry to Jack
As they slogged up to Arras with rifle and pack.

But he did for them both by his plan of attack.

Does it Matter?

Does it matter? – losing your legs?...
For people will always be kind,
And you need not show that you mind
When the others come in after hunting
To gobble their muffins and eggs.

Does it matter? – losing your sight?...
There's such splendid work for the blind;
And people will always be kind,
As you sit on the terrace remembering
And turning your face to the light.

Do they matter? – those dreams from the pit?...
You can drink and forget and be glad,
And people won't say that you're mad;
For they'll know you've fought for your country
And no one will worry a bit.

Survivors

No doubt they'll soon get well; the shock and strain
    Have caused their stammering, disconnected talk.
Of course they're 'longing to go out again,' –
    These boys with old, scared faces, learning to walk.
They'll soon forget their haunted nights; their cowed
    Subjection to the ghosts of friends who died, –
Their dreams that drip with murder; and they'll be proud
    Of glorious war that shatter'd all their pride...
Men who went out to battle, grim and glad;
Children, with eyes that hate you, broken and mad.

I Stood with the Dead

I stood with the Dead, so forsaken and still:
When dawn was grey I stood with the Dead.
And my slow heart said, 'You must kill, you must kill:
Soldier, soldier, morning is red'.

On the shapes of the slain in their crumpled disgrace
I stared for a while through the thin cold rain...
'O lad that I loved, there is rain on your face,
And your eyes are blurred and sick like the plain.'

I stood with the Dead...They were dead; they were dead;
My heart and my head beat a march of dismay:
And gusts of the wind came dulled by the guns.
'Fall in!' I shouted; 'Fall in for your pay!'

Everyone Sang

Everyone suddenly burst out singing;
And I was filled with such delight
As prisoned birds must find in freedom,
Winging wildly across the white
Orchards and dark-green fields; on – on – and out of sight.

Everyone's voice was suddenly lifted;
And beauty came like the setting sun:
My heart was shaken with tears; and horror
Drifted away... O, but Everyone
Was a bird; and the song was wordless; the singing will
     never be done.

Mary Borden
1886 – 1968

Mary ('May') Borden, later Lady Spears, was born in Chicago. Her father died when she was 20, leaving her independently wealthy. She published her first novel in 1912, when she settled in London with her husband and three children. She became a popular figure in literary circles.

During a suffragette protest in 1913 Borden was arrested and then imprisoned for throwing a stone through a window of the Treasury. On the outbreak of war she volunteered to serve as a nurse with the French Red Cross. She subsequently funded and ran her own military field hospital for wounded French soldiers, as close to the front line as possible (something she did again in the Second World War). When Captain (later General) Louis Spears visited her hospital on the Somme, they fell in love and later married. She lost much of her fortune in the years following the Wall Street Crash.

She wrote of her wartime experience in *The Forbidden Zone* (1929): 'It was my business to know which of the wounded could wait and which could not. I had to decide for myself. There was no one to tell me. If I made any mistakes, some would die on their stretchers on the floor under my eyes who need not have died [...] My hands could instantly tell the difference between the cold of the harsh bitter night and the stealthy cold of death.'

The Song of the Mud

This is the song of the mud,
The pale yellow glistening mud that covers the hills like
    satin;
The grey gleaming silvery mud that is spread like enamel
    over the valleys;
The frothing, squirting, spurting, liquid mud that gurgles
    along the road beds;
The thick elastic mud that is kneaded and pounded and
    squeezed under the hoofs of the horses;
The invincible, inexhaustible mud of the war zone.

This is the song of the mud, the uniform of the poilu.
His coat is of mud, his great dragging flapping coat, that is
    too big for him and too heavy;
His coat that once was blue and now is grey and stiff with
    the mud that cakes to it.
This is the mud that clothes him.
His trousers and boots are of mud,
And his skin is of mud;
And there is mud in his beard.
His head is crowned with a helmet of mud.
He wears it well.
He wears it as a king wears the ermine that bores him.
He has set a new style in clothing;
He has introduced the chic of mud.

This is the song of the mud that wriggles its way into battle.
The impertinent, the intrusive, the ubiquitous, the
    unwelcome,
The slimy inveterate nuisance,
That fills the trenches,
That mixes in with the food of the soldiers,
That spoils the working of motors and crawls into their
    secret parts,
That spreads itself over the guns,
That sucks the guns down and holds them fast in its slimy
    voluminous lips,
That has no respect for destruction and muzzles the bursting
    shells;
And slowly, softly, easily,
Soaks up the fire, the noise; soaks up the energy and the
    courage;
Soaks up the power of armies;
Soaks up the battle.
Just soaks it up and thus stops it.

This is the hymn of mud – the obscene, the filthy, the putrid,
The vast liquid grave of our armies.
It has drowned our men.
Its monstrous distended belly reeks with the undigested
    dead.
Our men have gone into it, sinking slowly, and struggling
    and slowly disappearing.
Our fine men, our brave, strong, young men;
Our glowing red, shouting, brawny men.
Slowly, inch by inch, they have gone down into it,

Into its darkness, its thickness, its silence.
Slowly, irresistibly, it drew them down, sucked them down,
And they were drowned in thick, bitter, heaving mud.
Now it hides them, Oh, so many of them!
Under its smooth glistening surface it is hiding them
    blandly.
There is not a trace of them.
There is no mark where they went down.
The mute enormous mouth of the mud has closed over
    them.

This is the song of the mud,
The beautiful glistening golden mud that covers the hills
    like satin;
The mysterious gleaming silvery mud that is spread like
    enamel over the valleys.
Mud, the disguise of the war zone;
Mud, the mantle of battles;
Mud, the smooth fluid grave of our soldiers:
This is the song of the mud.

No, no! There is some sinister mistake

No, no! There is some sinister mistake.
You cannot love me now. I am no more
A thing to touch, a pleasant thing to take
Into one's arms. How can a man adore
A woman with black blood upon her face,
A cap of horror on her pallid head,
Mirrors of madness in the sunken place
Of eyes; hands dripping with the slimy dead?
Go. Cover close your proud untainted brow.
Go quickly. Leave me to the hungry lust
Of monstrous pain. I am his mistress now –
These are the frantic beds of his delight –
Here I succumb to him, anew, each night.

Handwritten draft

See how the withered leaves

See how the withered leaves lie shivering
Along the gutters of the autumn street.
They are the souls of women; quivering
Shrivelled souls of women who once were sweet
To the desiring lips of hungry men.
Now they adorn the road where pleasure rides
Poor withered things – Yes, kiss me once again
Who knows what bitterness the future hides?
Kiss me until you've kissed my mouth away
Wear out my flesh with your enamoured hands
Drink up my heart beats, one by one and say
That I have satisfied your fierce demands –
Ah look, the frightened leaves are fluttering
Before the wind, the wind that's muttering.

Handwritten draft

Come to me quickly and take me away

Come to me quickly and take me away from my wounded
     men –
I cannot bear their pain anymore –
Come quickly and take me away out of this place
Give me rest, give me strength, give me cleanness and joy for
     one hour.
I am suffocating –
I cannot get away –
They cling to my skirts, my arms
My hands –
They clutch at my strength
They call my name – They keep calling me.
They cry to me to undo their pain and let them free –
     I cannot set them free.
They throw themselves onto my breast, to die –
I cannot even let them die –
Come to me for one hour, strong, clean – whole –
Their wounds gape at me –
Their stumps menace me –
Their bandaged faces grimace at me
Their death rattle curses me –
Give me rest – Make me clean
I am stained – I am soiled –
I am streaked with their blood –
I am soaked with the odor of the oozing of their wounds –
I am saturated with the poison of their poor festering
     wounds –

I am poisoned – I'm infected – I shall never wash it off –
But you are clean –
Your face is cold and fresh and wet by the rain –
Let me drink the fresh moisture of your face with my lips –
Your garments are electric with the wild blowing wind –
Put your gallant cloak about me –
Let me breathe, Let me breathe –
Give me rest –
Take me in your arms, your strong accustomed arms and
     swing me up and hold me close and quietly oh quietly
     set me afloat upon your tenderness
That I may be light light –
For I am heavy with the weight of my helpless wounded
     men –
I can bear no more the weight of their rolling heads, their
     broken limbs, their inert bodies.
Give me strength –
Stop the shaking of my hands –
I am shaking – I cannot keep from shaking
I am shaking because I have had to be strong for so long.
When they clung to me I held them –
When they tossed I held them still –
When they fought I held them down –
When they clutched at me, sinking, drowning in their agony,
     I held them.
Oh how I tried to hold them up and save them.
But their pain was so strong that it has left me shaking.
I can't hold them any more –
Give me strength –
And give me joy –

I emplore you – I beseech you – Give me joy for one hour –
That I may go back again to comfort them.
Take me out through the dark and up the hill
Where the wind and the roar of cannon surge and beat
    about us –
Where the flares run red through the wide luminous
    blackness –
There speak to me quietly – you who have never failed me –
Say my name with confidence
Repeat my name to me –
The sound of your voice saying my name
Assures me that I have always sufficed you.
Listen – I hear their delirium calling.
Speak to me quietly –
Let the war thunder –
Tell me that in our house the chimney fires are burning –
The quiet rooms are waiting.
And the tall trees are protecting the place that we have left,
    the place where we will go, again, someday.
Hold me still and let me listen to the faint far echoing music
    of the youth we had together –
Hold me and let me hear the chanting of the years, all the
    years that you have loved me, the sure deep splendid
    years, with you who never failed me –
Ah, you who have always loved me,
Come to me for an hour
Then let me go back to my wounded men

From an early, handwritten draft of The Forbidden Zone

Unidentified

Look well at this man. Look!
Come up out of your graves, philosophers,
And you who founded churches, and all you
Who for ten thousand years have talked of God.
Come out of your uncomfortable tombs, astronomers,
Who raked the heavens with your mighty eyes,
And died, unanswered questions on your lips,
For you have something interesting to learn
By looking at this man.

Stand all about, you many-legioned ghosts;
Fill up the desert with your shadowy forms,
And in the vast resounding waste of death,
Watch him while he dies;
He will not notice you.

Observe his ugliness.
See how he stands there planted in the mud like some old
     battered image of a faith forgotten by its God.
Note his naked neck and jutting jaw under the iron hat
     that's jammed upon his head;
See how he rounds his shoulders, bends his back inside his
     clumsy coat;
And how he leans ahead, gripping with grimy fists
The muzzle of his gun that digs it butt-end down into the
     mud between the solid columns of his legs.

Look close, come close, pale ghosts!

Come back out of the dim unfinished past;

Crowd up across the edges of the earth,

Where the horizon, like a red hot wire, twists underneath
tremendous smoking blows.

Come up, come up across the quaking ground that gapes in
sudden holes beneath your feet;

Come fearlessly across the twisting field where bones of men
stick through the tortured mud.

Ghosts have no need to fear.

Look close at this man. Look !

He waits for death;

He watches it approach;

His little bloodshot eyes can see it bearing down on every
side;

He feels it coming underneath his feet, running, burrowing
underneath the ground;

He hears it screaming in the frantic air.

Death that tears the shrieking sky in two,

That suddenly explodes out of the festering bowels of the
earth –

Dreadful and horrid death.

He takes the impact of it on his back, his chest, his
belly and his arms;

Spreads his legs upon its lurching form;

Plants his feet upon its face and breathes deep into his
pumping lungs the gassy breath of death.

He does not move.

In all the running landscape there's a solitary thing that's
      motionless:
The figure of this man.

The sky long since has fallen from its dome.
Terror let loose like a gigantic wind has torn it from the
      ceiling of the world,
And it is flapping down in frantic shreds.
The earth ages ago leaped screaming up out of the fastness
      of its ancient laws.
There is no centre now to hold it down.
It rolls and writhes, a shifting tortured thing, a floating mass
      of matter set adrift.
And in between the fluttering tatters of the ruined sky,
And the convulsions of the maddened earth,
The man stands solid.
Something holds him there.

What holds him, timid ghosts?
What do you say, you shocked and shuddering ghosts,
Dragged from your sheltered vaults;
You who once died in quiet lamp-lit rooms;
Who were companioned to the end by friends;
And closed your eyes in languor on a world
That you had fashioned for your pleasant selves?
You scorned this man.
He was for you an ordinary man.
Some of you pitied him, prayed over his soul, worried him
      with stories of Heaven and Hell.
Promised him Heaven if he would be ashamed of being
      what he was,

And everlasting sorrow if he died as he had lived, an
     ordinary man.
You gave him Gods he could not know, and images of God;
     laws he could not keep, and punishment.
You were afraid of him.
Everything about him that was his very own
Made you afraid of him.
His love of women, food and drink, and fun,
His clumsy reach for life, his open grabbing fist,
His stupid open gaping heart and mouth.
He was a hungry man,
And you were afraid of him.
None of you trusted him;
No one of you was his friend.

Look at him now. Look well, look long.
Your hungry brute, your ordinary man;
Your fornicator, drunkard, anarchist;
Your ruthless rough seed-sowing male;
Your angry greedy egotist;
Your lost, bewildered, childish dunce;
Come close and look into his haggard face.
It is too late to do him justice now, or even speak to him.
But look.
Look at the stillness of his face.
It's made of little fragile bones and flesh, tissued of quivering
     muscles fine as silk;
Exquisite nerves, soft membrane warm with blood,
That travels smoothly through the tender veins.

One blow, one minute more, and that man's face will be a
    mass of matter, horrid slime and little brittle splinters.
He knows.
He waits.
His face remains quite still.
And underneath the bullet-spattered helmet on his head
His steady eyes look out.
What is it that looks out?
What is deep mirrored in those bloodshot eyes?
Terror? No.
Despair? Perhaps.
What else?
Ah, poor ghosts – poor blind unseeing ghosts!
It is his self you see;
His self that does remember what he loved and what he
    wanted, and what he never had;
His self that can regret, that can reproach its own self now;
    his self that gave itself, let loose its hold of all but just
    itself.
Is that, then, nothing? Just his naked self, pinning down a
    shaking world,
A single rivet driven down to hold a universe together.

Go back, poor ghosts. Go back into your graves.
He has no use for you, this nameless man.
Scholars, philosophers, men of God, leave this man alone.
No lamp you lit will show his soul the way;
No name restore his lost identity.
The guns will chant his death march down the world;
The flare of cannon light his dying;
The mute and nameless men beneath his feet will welcome
    him beside them in the mud.
Take one last look and leave him standing there,
Unfriended, unrewarded, and unknown.

Geoffrey Studdert Kennedy

1883 – 1929

Geoffrey Studdert Kennedy grew up in Leeds and studied at Trinity College, Dublin. He was ordained in the Church of England and in 1915 volunteered as an army chaplain. Based at the front, he helped with the wounded, acting as a stretcher-bearer and medical aide. He comforted the dying and buried the dead, often where they had fallen. He gained the nickname 'Woodbine Willie' for his habit of handing out cigarettes to cheer up the men, saying a chaplain needed 'a box of fags in your haversack, and a great deal of love in your heart'.

Gregarious, funny and unconventional, he was a popular preacher at a time when many men had abandoned their faith ('I know what you're thinking, here comes the bloody parson'). He was awarded the Military Cross for a particular act of bravery on the battlefield, which he himself described: 'There was no morphine. That was the horror. Someone must go for it. I went. I went because the hell outside was less awful than the hell in. I didn't go to do an heroic deed or perform a Christian service; I went because I couldn't bear the moaning any longer.'

His populist poetry is reminiscent of Kipling's ballads and seeks to give voice to the ordinary men he served. Later he was a chaplain to the king, and a missionary to working class communities.

His Mate

There's a broken, battered village
    Somewhere up behind the line,
There's a dug-out and a bunk there,
    That I used to say were mine.

I remember how I reached them,
    Dripping wet and all forlorn,
In the dim and dreary twilight
    Of a weeping summer morn.

All that week I'd buried brothers,
    In one bitter battle slain,
In one grave I laid two hundred.
    God! What sorrow and what rain!

And that night I'd been in trenches,
    Seeking out the sodden dead,
And just dropping them in shell-holes,
    With a service swiftly said.

For the bullets rattled round me,
    But I couldn't leave them there,
Water-soaked in flooded shell-holes,
    Reft of common Christian prayer.

So I crawled round on my belly,
    And I listened to the roar
Of the guns that hammered Thiepval,
    Like big breakers on the shore.

Then there spoke a dripping sergeant,
    When the time was growing late,
"Would you please to bury this one,
    'Cause 'e used to be my mate?"

So we groped our way in darkness
    To a body lying there,
Just a blacker lump of blackness,
    With a red blotch on his hair.

Though we turned him gently over,
    Yet I still can hear the thud,
As the body fell face forward,
    And then settled in the mud.

We went down upon our faces,
    And I said the service through,
From "I am the Resurrection,"
    To the last, the great "adieu."

We stood up to give the Blessing,
    And commend him to the Lord,
When a sudden light shot soaring
    Silver swift and like a sword.

At a stroke it slew the darkness,
    Flashed its glory on the mud,
And I saw the sergeant staring
    At a crimson clot of blood.

There are many kinds of sorrow
  In this world of Love and Hate,
But there is no sterner sorrow
  Than a soldier's for his mate.

To Stretcher-Bearers

Easy does it – bit o' trench 'ere,
Mind that blinkin' bit o' wire,
There's a shell 'ole on your left there,
Lift 'im up a little 'igher.
Stick it, lad, ye'll soon be there now,
Want to rest 'ere for a while?
Let 'im dahn then – gently – gently,
There ye are, lad. That's the style.
Want a drink, mate? 'Ere's my bottle,
Lift 'is 'ead up for 'im, Jack,
Put my tunic underneath 'im,
'Ow's that, chummy? That's the tack!
Guess we'd better make a start now,
Ready for another spell?
Best be goin', we won't 'urt ye,
But 'e might just start to shell.
Are ye right, mate? Off we goes then.
That's well over on the right;
Gawd Almighty, that's a near 'un!
'Old your end up good and tight,
Never mind, lad, you're for Blighty.
Mind this rotten bit o' board.

We'll soon 'ave ye tucked in bed, lad,
'Opes ye gets to my old ward.
No more war for you, my 'earty,
This'll get ye well away,
Twelve good months in dear old Blighty,
Twelve good months if you're a day.
M.O.'s got a bit o' something
What'll stop that blarsted pain.
'Ere's a rotten bit o' ground, mate,
Lift up 'igher – up again,
Wish 'e'd stop 'is blarsted shellin',
Makes it rotten for the lad.
When a feller's been and got it,
It affec's 'im twice as bad.
'Ow's it goin' now then, sonny?
'Ere's that narrow bit o' trench,
Careful, mate, there's some dead Jerries.
Gawd Almighty, what a stench!
'Ere we are now, stretcher-case, boys,
Bring him aht a cup o' tea!
Inasmuch as ye have done it
Ye have done it unto Me.

Old England

Yes, I'm fightin' for old England
  And for eighteenpence a day,
And I'm fightin' like an 'ero,
  So the daily papers say.
Well, I ain't no downy chicken,
  I'm a bloke past forty-three,
And I'm goin' to tell ye honest
  What old England means to me.
When I joined the British Army
  I'd bin workin' thirty years,
But I left my bloomin' rent book
  Showin' three months in arrears.
No, I weren't no chronic boozer,
  Nor I weren't a lad to bet;
I worked 'ard when I could get it,
  And I weren't afeared to sweat.
But I weren't a tradesman proper,
  And the work were oft to seek,
So the most as I could addle
  Were abaht a quid a week.
And when me and Jane got married,
  And we 'ad our oldest kid,
We soon learned 'ow many shillings
  Go to make a golden quid.
For we 'ad to keep our clubs up,
  And there's three and six for rent,
And with food and boots and clothing
  It no sooner came than went.

Then when kiddies kep' on comin' –
  We reared four and buried three;
My ole woman couldn't do it,
  So we got in debt – ye see.
And we 'ad a 'eap o' sickness
  And we got struck off the club,
With our little lot o' troubles
  We just couldn't pay the sub.
No, I won't tell you no false'oods;
  There were times I felt that queer,
That I went and did the dirty,
  And I 'ad a drop o' beer.
Then the wife and me 'ud quarrel,
  And our 'ome were little 'ell,
Wiv the 'ungry kiddies cryin',
  Till I eased up for a spell.
There were times when it were better,
  And some times when it were worse,
But to take it altogether,
  My old England were a curse.
It were sleepin', sweatin', starvin',
  Wearing boot soles for a job,
It were sucking up to foremen
  What 'ud sell ye for a bob.
It were cringin', crawlin', whinin',
  For the right to earn your bread,
It were schemin', pinchin', plannin',
  It were wishin' ye was dead.
I'm not fightin' for old England,
  Not for this child – am I? 'Ell!

For the sake o' that old England
    I'd not face a single shell,
Not a single bloomin' whizzbang.
    Never mind this blarsted show,
With your comrades fallin' round ye,
    Lyin' bleedin' in a row.
This ain't war, it's ruddy murder,
    It s a stinkin' slaughter 'ouse.
'Ark to that one, if 'e got ye
    'E'd just squash ye like this louse.
Would I do this for old England,
    Would I? 'Ell, I says, not me!
What I says is, sink old England
    To the bottom of the sea!
It's new England as I fights for,
    It's an England swep' aht clean,
It's an England where we'll get at
    Things our eyes 'ave never seen;
Decent wages, justice, mercy,
    And a chance for ev'ry man
For to make 'is 'ome an 'eaven
    If 'e does the best 'e can.
It's that better, cleaner England,
    Made o' better, cleaner men,
It's that England as I fights for,
    And I'm game to fight again.
It's the better land o' Blighty
    That still shines afore our eyes,
That's the land a soldier fights for,
    And for that a soldier dies.

Demobilised

Out through its curtain of dark blue mist,
Glittering gold where the sun has kissed,
Out till it reaches the shining sea,
Stretches the land that is home to me;
Valley and hillock and wooded copse,
Promise of wealth in the fresh green crops.
Mother of Mothers that gave me birth,
Bone of my bone is thy rich red earth,
Flesh of my flesh is thy land to me,
The land that ends in the shining sea.

Mother, I come from a wounded land,
Where the earth is torn and the poor trees stand
Like naked masts, black – stiff – and stark,
Over the grave of some gallant bark;
Where peasant's cottage and nobles' halls
Are heaps of brick or the four bare walls,
With lonely graves in a maze of wire,
Where stood the church with its peaceful spire.
Out of the ruin I come to thee,
Hail, Mother mine, by the shining sea.

Dear to me ever thy country-side,
But dearer now for the men who died,
Robbed of the richest of youth's long years,
Steeling their hearts to a mother's tears,
Fighting their way through a thousand hells,
Bearing a cross like a cap and bells,
Jeering at death as a last good joke.

My thanks go up with the thin blue smoke,
Marking the cottage that's home to me,
In the dear safe land by the shining sea.

Edward Thomas

1878 – 1917

Edward Thomas grew up in London. He studied History at Oxford, and earned his living as a writer. His closely observed, lyrical descriptions of the English countryside (*The South Country*, *In Pursuit of Spring*) express a deep passion for the natural world.

He joined the ranks of the Artists' Rifles in 1915 and initially worked as a map instructor before he was commissioned into the Royal Artillery. He embarked for France in January 1917 and was killed on 9 April, by a shell blast. Thomas only began writing poems at the outbreak of war, which coincided for him with an outburst of creativity, encouraged by his friend and fellow poet Robert Frost. He was out of sympathy with popular nationalism, and was ambivalent about the conflict itself. When asked why he chose to enlist at the age of 37, he bent down to pick up a handful of English soil and said, 'Literally, for this'.

Thomas's war diary contains detailed observations of both the war and nature, and notes for the future poems and books he hoped to write. On 23 February he described life in a small French town destroyed by shells: 'Wet, mortar, litter, almanacs, bottles, broken glass, damp beds, dirty paper, knife, crucifix, statuette, old chairs. Our cat moves with the Group wherever it goes […] 2 owls in garden at 6. The shelling must have slaughtered many jackdaws but has made home for many more.'

In Memoriam (Easter, 1915)

The flowers left thick at nightfall in the wood
This Eastertide call into mind the men,
Now far from home, who, with their sweethearts, should
Have gathered them and will do never again.

This is no case of petty right or wrong

This is no case of petty right or wrong
That politicians or philosophers
Can judge. I hate not Germans, nor grow hot
With love of Englishmen, to please newspapers.
Beside my hate for one fat patriot
My hatred of the Kaiser is love true: –
A kind of god he is, banging a gong.
But I have not to choose between the two,
Or between justice and injustice. Dinned
With war and argument I read no more
Than in the storm smoking along the wind
Athwart the wood. Two witches' cauldrons roar.
From one the weather shall rise clear and gay;
Out of the other an England beautiful
And like her mother that died yesterday.
Little I know or care if, being dull,
I shall miss something that historians
Can rake out of the ashes when perchance
The phoenix broods serene above their ken.
But with the best and meanest Englishmen

I am one in crying, God save England, lest
We lose what never slaves and cattle blessed.
The ages made her that made us from the dust:
She is all we know and live by, and we trust
She is good and must endure, loving her so:
And as we love ourselves we hate her foe.

Rain

Rain, midnight rain, nothing but the wild rain
On this bleak hut, and solitude, and me
Remembering again that I shall die
And neither hear the rain nor give it thanks
For washing me cleaner than I have been
Since I was born into this solitude.
Blessed are the dead that the rain rains upon:
But here I pray that none whom once I loved
Is dying tonight or lying still awake
Solitary, listening to the rain,
Either in pain or thus in sympathy
Helpless among the living and the dead,
Like a cold water among broken reeds,
Myriads of broken reeds all still and stiff,
Like me who have no love which this wild rain
Has not dissolved except the love of death,
If love it be towards what is perfect and
Cannot, the tempest tells me, disappoint.

'Home'

Fair was the morning, fair our tempers, and
We had seen nothing fairer than that land,
Though strange, and the untrodden snow that made
Wild of the tame, casting out all that was
Not wild and rustic and old; and we were glad.

Fair, too, was afternoon, and first to pass
Were we that league of snow, next the north wind.
There was nothing to return for, except need,
And yet we sang nor ever stopped for speed,
As we did often with the start behind.
Faster still strode we when we came in sight
Of the cold roofs where we must spend the night.
Happy we had not been there, nor could be,
Though we had tasted sleep and food and fellowship
Together long.
   'How quick' to someone's lip
The words came, 'will the beaten horse run home.'

The word 'home' raised a smile in us all three,
And one repeated it, smiling just so
That all knew what he meant and none would say.
Between three counties far apart that lay
We were divided and looked strangely each
At the other, and we knew we were not friends
But fellows in a union that ends
With the necessity for it, as it ought.

Never a word was spoken, not a thought
Was thought, of what the look meant with the word
'Home' as we walked and watched the sunset blurred.
And then to me the word, only the word,
'Homesick', as it were playfully occurred:
No more.

        If I should ever more admit
Than the mere word I could not endure it
For a day longer: this captivity
Must somehow come to an end, else I should be
Another man, as often now I seem,
Or this life be only an evil dream.

The Cherry Trees

The cherry trees bend over and are shedding
On the old road where all that passed are dead,
Their petals, strewing the grass as for a wedding
This early May morn when there is none to wed.

The sun used to shine

The sun used to shine while we two walked
Slowly together, paused and started
Again, and sometimes mused, sometimes talked
As either pleased, and cheerfully parted

Each night. We never disagreed
Which gate to rest on. The to be
And the late past we gave small heed.
We turned from men or poetry

To rumours of the war remote
Only till both stood disinclined
For aught but the yellow flavorous coat
Of an apple wasps had undermined;

Or a sentry of dark betonies,
The stateliest of small flowers on earth,
At the forest verge; or crocuses
Pale purple as if they had their birth

In sunless Hades fields. The war
Came back to mind with the moonrise
Which soldiers in the east afar
Beheld then. Nevertheless, our eyes

Could as well imagine the Crusades
Or Caesar's battles. Everything
To faintness like those rumours fades –
Like the brook's water glittering

Under the moonlight – like those walks
Now – like us two that took them, and
The fallen apples, all the talks
And silences – like memory's sand

When the tide covers it late or soon,
And other men through other flowers
In those fields under the same moon
Go talking and have easy hours.

The Trumpet

Rise up, rise up,
And, as the trumpet blowing
Chases the dreams of men,
As the dawn glowing
The stars that left unlit
The land and water,
Rise up and scatter
The dew that covers
The print of last night's lovers –
Scatter it, scatter it!

While you are listening
To the clear horn,
Forget, men, everything
On this earth newborn,
Except that it is lovelier
Than any mysteries.
Open your eyes to the air

That has washed the eyes of the stars
Through all the dewy night:
Up with the light,
To the old wars;
Arise, arise!

As the team's head-brass

As the team's head-brass flashed out on the turn
The lovers disappeared into the wood.
I sat among the boughs of the fallen elm
That strewed an angle of the fallow, and
Watched the plough narrowing a yellow square
Of charlock. Every time the horses turned
Instead of treading me down, the ploughman leaned
Upon the handles to say or ask a word,
About the weather, next about the war.
Scraping the share he faced towards the wood,
And screwed along the furrow till the brass flashed
Once more.
          The blizzard felled the elm whose crest
I sat in, by a woodpecker's round hole,
The ploughman said. 'When will they take it away?'
'When the war's over.' So the talk began –
One minute and an interval of ten,
A minute more and the same interval.
'Have you been out?' 'No.' 'And don't want to, perhaps?'
'If I could only come back again, I should.
I could spare an arm. I shouldn't want to lose

A leg. If I should lose my head, why, so,
I should want nothing more.... Have many gone
From here?' 'Yes.' 'Many lost?' 'Yes: a good few.
Only two teams work on the farm this year.
One of my mates is dead. The second day
In France they killed him. It was back in March,
The very night of the blizzard, too. Now if
He had stayed here we should have moved the tree.'
'And I should not have sat here. Everything
Would have been different. For it would have been
Another world.' 'Ay, and a better, though
If we could see all all might seem good.' Then
The lovers came out of the wood again:
The horses started and for the last time
I watched the clods crumble and topple over
After the ploughshare and the stumbling team.

No one cares less than I

'No one cares less than I,
Nobody knows but God,
Whether I am destined to lie
Under a foreign clod,'
Were the words I made to the bugle call in the morning.

But laughing, storming, scorning,
Only the bugles know
What the bugles say in the morning,
And they do not care, when they blow
The call that I heard and made words to early this morning.

Lights Out

I have come to the borders of sleep,
The unfathomable deep
Forest where all must lose
Their way, however straight,
Or winding, soon or late;
They cannot choose.

Many a road and track
That, since the dawn's first crack,
Up to the forest brink,
Deceived the travellers
Suddenly now blurs,
And in they sink.

Here love ends,
Despair, ambition ends,
All pleasure and all trouble,
Although most sweet or bitter,
Here ends in sleep that is sweeter
Than tasks most noble.

There is not any book
Or face of dearest look
That I would not turn from now
To go into the unknown
I must enter and leave alone,
I know not how.

The tall forest towers;
Its cloudy foliage lowers
Ahead, shelf above shelf;
Its silence I hear and obey
That I may lose my way
And myself.

David Jones
1895 – 1974

David Jones grew up in Kent and studied at the Camberwell School of Art. His slight build initially made it difficult for him to enlist, but in early 1915 he joined the Royal Welch Fusiliers, the same regiment as Sassoon and Graves. Unlike them he served as a private. His intelligence and middle class accent brought about the question of applying for a commission, but he seems to have preferred the ranks. He was in the trenches for longer than any other major soldier-poet (117 weeks) and later said that, unlike Wilfred Owen, he believed in 'the old lie'. After being wounded at the Somme he wrote: 'The trench is still cold and wet; eyes still ache, and hands freeze. But it's worth it!' His work was strongly influenced by his Roman Catholic faith, as well as by Welsh and Arthurian mythology, and Roman and early British history, as he sought to connect his own experience to a greater historical and divine context.

Jones worked with artist Eric Gill for a number of years. He is a significant figure among British Modernists for his drawings, engravings and paintings, as well as for his poetry, with its characteristic fusion of verse and prose. This excerpt from *In Parenthesis* describes the attack on Mametz Wood, during which he received 'a Blighty', a bullet wound which meant he was sent home for a few weeks.

excerpts from In Parenthesis, Part 7

The gentle slopes are green to remind you
of South English places, only far wider and flatter spread
and grooved and harrowed criss-cross whitely and the
disturbed subsoil heaped up albescent.

Across upon this undulated board of verdure chequered
bright
when you look to left and right
small, drab, bundled pawns severally make effort
moved in tenuous line
and if you looked behind – the next wave came slowly, as
successive surfs creep in to dissipate on flat shore;
and to your front, stretched long laterally,
and receed deeply,
the dark wood.

*

Mr. Jenkins half inclined his head to them – he walked just
barely in advance of his platoon and immediately to the left
of Private Ball.
    He makes the conventional sign
and there is the deeply inward effort of spent men who
would make response for him,
and take it at the double.
He sinks on one knee
and now on the other,
his upper body tilts in rigid inclination
this way and back;

weighted lanyard runs out to full tether,
>   swings like a pendulum
>   and the clock run down.
Lurched over, jerked iron saucer over tilted brow,
clampt unkindly over lip and chin
nor no ventaille to this darkening
>   and masked face lifts to grope the air
and so disconsolate;
enfeebled fingering at a paltry strap –
buckle holds,
holds him blind against the morning.

   Then stretch still where weeds pattern the chalk predella
– where it rises to his wire – and Sergeant T. Quilter takes
over.

Sergeant Quilter is shouting his encouragements, you can
almost hear him, he opens his mouth so wide.
   Sergeant Quilter breaks into double-time
and so do the remainder.
   You stumble in a place of tentacle
you seek a place made straight
you unreasonably blame the artillery
you stand waist-deep
you stand upright
you stretch out hands to pluck at Jerry wire as if it were
bramble mesh.

No. 3 section inclined a little right where a sequence of
9.2's have done well their work of preparation and cratered
a plain passage. They bunch, a bewildered half dozen, like
sheep where the wall is tumbled – but high-perched

Brandenburgers
from their leafy vantage-tops observe
that kind of folly:
nevertheless, you and one other walk alive before his
parapets.

Yet a taut prehensile strand gets you at the instep, even so,
and sprawls you useless to the First Objective. But Private
Watcyn takes it with blameless technique, and even
remembers to halloo the official blasphemies.

The inorganic earth where your body presses seems itself
to pulse deep down with your heart's acceleration...
but you go on living, lying with your face bedded in neatly
folded, red-piped, greatcoat and yet no cold cleaving thing
drives in between expectant shoulder-blades, so you get
to your feet, and the sun-lit chalk is everywhere absorbing
fresh stains.

Dark gobbets stiffen skewered to revetment-hurdles and
dyed garments strung-up for a sign;

but the sun shines also
on the living
and on Private Watcyn, who wears a strange look under his
iron brim, like a small child caught at some bravado in a
garden, and old Dawes comes so queerly from the thing he
saw in the next bay but one.

But for all that it is relatively pleasant here under the first
trees and lying in good cover.

But Sergeant Quilter is already on the parados. He sorts
them out a bit
they are five of No. 1
six of No. 2

two of No. 3
four of No. 4
a lance-jack, and a corporal.
    So these nineteen deploy
between the rowan and the hazel,
go forward to the deeper shades.

And now all the wood-ways live with familiar faces and your
mate moves like Jack o' the Green: for this season's fertility
gone unpruned, & this year's renewing sap shot up fresh
tendrils to cumber greenly the heaped decay of last fall, and
no forester to tend the paths, nor strike with axes to the root
of selected boles, nor had come Jacqueline to fill a pinafore
with may-thorn.
    But keepers who engineer new and powerful devices,
forewarned against this morning
prepared with booby-trap beneath
and platforms in the stronger branches
like main-top for an arbalestier,
precisely and competently advised and all in the know,
as to this hour
        when unicorns break cover
and come down
and foxes flee, whose warrens know the shock,
and birds complain in flight – for their nests fall like stars
        and all their airy world gone crazed
and the whole woodland rocks where these break their horns.

It was largely his machine guns in Acid Copse that did it,
and our own heavies firing by map reference, with all lines
phut and no reliable liaison.

So you just lay where you were and shielded what you could of your body.

It slackened a little and they try short rushes and you find yourself alone in a denseness of hazel-brush and body high bramble and between the bright interstices and multifarious green-stuff, grey textile, scarlet-edged goes and comes – and there is another withdrawing-heel from the thicket.

His light stick-bomb winged above your thorn-bush, and aged oak-timbers shiver and leaves shower like thrown blossom for a conqueror.

You tug at rusted pin –

it gives unexpectedly and your fingers pressed to released flange.

You loose the thing into the underbrush.

Dark-faceted iron oval lobs heavily to fungus-cushioned dank, wobbles under low leaf to lie, near where the heel drew out just now; and tough root-fibres boomerang to top-most green filigree and earth clods flung disturb fresh fragile shoots that brush the sky.

You huddle closer to your mossy bed

you make yourself scarce

you scramble forward and pretend not to see,

but ruby drops from young beech-sprigs –

are bright your hands and face.

And the other one cries from the breaking-buckthorn.

He calls for Elsa, for Manuela

for the parish priest of Burkersdorf in Saxe Altenburg.

You grab his dropt stick-bomb as you go, but somehow you don't fancy it and anyway you forget how it works. You definitely like the coloured label on the handle, you throw it to the tall wood-weeds.

So double detonations, back and fro like well-played-up-to service at a net, mark left and right the forcing of the groves.

*

But it's no good you cant do it with these toy spades, you want axes, heavy iron for tough anchoring roots, tendoned deep down.

When someone brought up the Jerry picks it was better, and you did manage to make some impression. And the next one to you, where he bends to delve gets it in the middle body. Private Ball is not instructed, and how could you stay so fast a tide, it would be difficult with him screaming whenever you move him ever so little, let alone try with jack-knife to cut clear the hampering cloth.

The First Field Dressing is futile as frantic seaman's shift bunged to stoved bulwark, so soon the darking flood percolates and he dies in your arms.

And get back to that digging can't yer –
this aint a bloody Wake
      for these dead, who soon will have their dead
for burial clods heaped over.
Nor time for halsing
nor to clip green wounds
nor weeping Maries bringing anointments
neither any word spoken

nor no decent nor appropriate sowing of this seed
nor remembrance of the harvesting
of the renascent cycle
and return
nor shaving of the head nor ritual incising for these *viriles*
under each tree.

    No one sings: Lully lully
for the mate whose blood runs down.

Isaac Rosenberg
1890 – 1918

Isaac Rosenberg grew up in poverty in Bristol and the East End of London. His father, a Lithuanian Jew, was a pedlar. At fourteen Rosenberg was reluctantly apprenticed to an engraver. His ambition was to be an artist and he studied at the Slade School of Art, with support from friends, including Edward Marsh. He went to South Africa in 1914 to seek a better climate for suspected tuberculosis. When he returned in 1915 he could find no work. Although not keen to enlist ('the idea of killing upsets me a bit'), he saw the Army as a source of income for himself and his mother. He had 'no patriotic convictions'. Because of his short stature he was assigned to a Bantam battalion, serving as a private. He was at the front for twenty-one months, with just ten days leave in that time. He experienced discrimination as a Jew in the ranks, and struggled to find time and paper for his writing. He was sometimes unable to send poems home because the censor 'won't be bothered with going through such rubbish'.

In January 1918 he wrote to Marsh: 'What is happening to me now is more tragic than the "passion play". Christ never endured what I endure. It is breaking me completely.' He was killed, probably in close combat, on 1 April. He lay unburied for many days until interred in a mass grave.

On Receiving News of the War: Cape Town

Snow is a strange white word.
No ice or frost
Have asked of bud or bird
For Winter's cost.

Yet ice and frost and snow
From earth to sky
This Summer land doth know.
No man knows why.

In all men's hearts it is.
Some spirit old
Hath turned with malign kiss
Our lives to mould.

Red fangs have torn His face.
God's blood is shed.
He mourns from His lone place
His children dead.

O! ancient crimson curse!
Corrode, consume.
Give back this universe
Its pristine bloom.

Marching – as seen from the left file

My eyes catch ruddy necks
Sturdily pressed back,–
All a red brick moving glint.
Like flaming pendulums, hands
Swing across the khaki –
Mustard-coloured khaki –
To the automatic feet.

We husband the ancient glory
In these bared necks and hands.
Not broke is the forge of Mars;
But a subtler brain beats iron
To shoe the hoofs of death,
(Who paws dynamic air now).
Blind fingers loose an iron cloud
To rain immortal darkness
On strong eyes.

The Troop Ship

Grotesque and queerly huddled
Contortionists to twist
The sleepy soul to a sleep,
We lie all sorts of ways
But cannot sleep.
The wet wind is so cold,
And the lurching men so careless,

That, should you drop to a doze,
Wind's fumble or men's feet
Is on your face.

In the Trenches

I snatched two poppies
From the parapet's edge,
Two bright red poppies
That winked on the ledge.
Behind my ear
I stuck one through,
One blood red poppy
I gave to you.

The sandbags narrowed
And screwed out our jest,
And tore the poppy
You had on your breast...
Down – a shell – O! Christ.
I am choked... safe... dust blind – I
See trench floor poppies
Strewn. Smashed you lie.

Break of Day in the Trenches

The darkness crumbles away.
It is the same old Druid Time as ever.
Only a live thing leaps my hand,
A queer sardonic rat,
As I pull the parapet's poppy
To stick behind my ear.
Droll rat, they would shoot you if they knew
Your cosmopolitan sympathies.
Now you have touched this English hand
You will do the same to a German
Soon, no doubt, if it be your pleasure
To cross the sleeping green between.
It seems, odd thing, you grin as you pass
Strong eyes, fine limbs, haughty athletes,
Less chanced than you for life,
Bonds to the whims of murder,
Sprawled in the bowels of the earth,
The torn fields of France.
What do you see in our eyes
At the shrieking iron and flame
Hurl'd through still heavens?
What quaver – what heart aghast?
Poppies whose roots are in man's veins
Drop, and are ever dropping,
But mine in my ear is safe –
Just a little white with the dust.

August 1914

What in our lives is burnt
In the fire of this?
The heart's dear granary?
The much we shall miss?

Three lives hath one life –
Iron, honey, gold.
The gold, the honey gone –
Left is the hard and cold.

Iron are our lives
Molten right through our youth.
A burnt space through ripe fields,
A fair mouth's broken tooth.

Louse Hunting

Nudes – stark aglisten
Yelling in lurid glee. Grinning faces of fiends
And raging limbs
Whirl over the floor one fire,
For a shirt verminously busy
Yon soldier tore from his throat
With oaths
Godhead might shrink at, but not the lice.
And soon the shirt was aflare
Over the candle he'd lit while we lay.
Then we all sprung up and stript
To hunt the vermin brood.

Soon like a demons' pantomime
The place was raging.
See the silhouettes agape,
See the gibbering shadows
Mixed with the battled arms on the wall.
See gargantuan hooked fingers
Dug in supreme flesh
To smutch the supreme littleness.
See the merry limbs in hot Highland fling
Because some wizard vermin
Charmed from the quiet this revel
When our ears were half lulled
By the dark music
Blown from Sleep's trumpet.

Returning, we hear the larks

Sombre the night is.
And though we have our lives, we know
What sinister threat lurks there.

Dragging these anguished limbs, we only know
This poison-blasted track opens on our camp –
On a little safe sleep.

But hark! joy – joy – strange joy.
Lo! heights of night ringing with unseen larks.
Music showering our upturned list'ning faces.

Death could drop from the dark
As easily as song –
But song only dropped,
Like a blind man's dreams on the sand
By dangerous tides,
Like a girl's dark hair for she dreams no ruin lies there,
Or her kisses where a serpent hides.

Dead Man's Dump

The plunging limbers over the shattered track
Racketed with their rusty freight,
Stuck out like many crowns of thorns,
And the rusty stakes like sceptres old
To stay the flood of brutish men
Upon our brothers dear.

The wheels lurched over sprawled dead
But pained them not, though their bones crunched,
Their shut mouths made no moan,
They lie there huddled, friend and foeman,
Man born of man, and born of woman,
And shells go crying over them
From night till night and now.

Earth has waited for them
All the time of their growth
Fretting for their decay:
Now she has them at last!
In the strength of their strength
Suspended – stopped and held.

What fierce imaginings their dark souls lit
Earth! have they gone into you?
Somewhere they must have gone,
And flung on your hard back
Is their soul's sack,
Emptied of God-ancestralled essences.
Who hurled them out? Who hurled?

None saw their spirits' shadow shake the grass,
Or stood aside for the half used life to pass
Out of those doomed nostrils and the doomed mouth,
When the swift iron burning bee
Drained the wild honey of their youth.

What of us, who flung on the shrieking pyre,
Walk, our usual thoughts untouched,
Our lucky limbs as on ichor fed,
Immortal seeming ever?
Perhaps when the flames beat loud on us,
A fear may choke in our veins
And the startled blood may stop.

The air is loud with death,
The dark air spurts with fire,
The explosions ceaseless are.

Timelessly now, some minutes past,
These dead strode time with vigorous life,
Till the shrapnel called 'an end!'
But not to all. In bleeding pangs
Some borne on stretchers dreamed of home,
Dear things, war-blotted from their hearts.

A man's brains splattered on
A stretcher-bearer's face;
His shook shoulders slipped their load,
But when they bent to look again
The drowning soul was sunk too deep
For human tenderness.

They left this dead with the older dead,
Stretched at the cross roads.

Burnt black by strange decay
Their sinister faces lie
The lid over each eye,
The grass and coloured clay
More motion have than they,
Joined to the great sunk silences.

Here is one not long dead;
His dark hearing caught our far wheels,
And the choked soul stretched weak hands
To reach the living word the far wheels said,
The blood-dazed intelligence beating for light,
Crying through the suspense of the far torturing wheels
Swift for the end to break,
Or the wheels to break,
Cried as the tide of the world broke over his sight.

Will they come? Will they ever come?
Even as the mixed hoofs of the mules,
The quivering-bellied mules,
And the rushing wheels all mixed
With his tortured upturned sight,
So we crashed round the bend,
We heard his weak scream,
We heard his very last sound,
And our wheels grazed his dead face.

Vera Brittain

1893 – 1970

In 1914 Vera Brittain was awarded
a scholarship to study English at
Somerville College, Oxford, 'won in
the teeth of family opposition', and
at a time when women were still not
permitted membership of the University itself. At the end of
her first year, she decided to suspend her studies and volunteer
as a nurse with the Voluntary Aid Detachment (VAD).

Brittain began her nursing career in London, before being
stationed in Malta, then France. Here she was at first posted
to care for German prisoners, an experience that affected her
deeply: 'the world was mad and we were all victims [...] these
shattered, dying boys and I were paying alike for a situation
that none of us had desired or done anything to bring about.'
She was to lose the people closest to her during the course of
the war, including her brother Edward and his school friend
Roland Leighton, with whom she was in love.

After the war she completed her studies, changing to
History so as to understand better how international politics
had led her generation 'through ignorance [...] to be used,
hypnotised and slaughtered'. After university she began a
distinguished career as a journalist, novelist and high-profile
campaigner for peace and women's rights. Her passionate and
thoughtful account of her wartime experiences, *Testament of
Youth* (1933), brought her international acclaim.

The German Ward

When the years of strife are over and my recollection fades
Of the wards wherein I worked the weeks away,
I shall still see as a vision rising through the wartime shades
The ward in France where German wounded lay.

I shall see the pallid faces and the half-suspicious eyes,
I shall hear the bitter groans and laboured breath,
And recall the loud complaining and the weary tedious cries,
And sights and smells of blood and wounds and death.

I shall see the convoy cases, blanket-covered on the floor,
And watch the heavy stretcher-work begin,
And the gleam of knives and bottles through the open
      theatre door,
And the operation patients carried in.

I shall see the Sister standing, with her form of youthful
      grace,
And the humour and the wisdom of her smile,
And the tale of three years' warfare on her thin expressive
      face –
The weariness of many a toil-filled while.

I shall think of how I worked for her with nerve and heart
      and mind,
And marvelled at her courage and her skill,
And how the dying enemy her tenderness would find
Beneath her scornful energy of will.

For I learnt that human mercy turns alike to friend or foe
When the darkest hour of all is creeping nigh,
And those who slew our dearest, when their lamps were
      burning low,
Found help and pity ere they came to die.

So though much will be forgotten when the sound of War's
      alarms
And the days of death and strife have passed away,
I shall always see the vision of Love working amidst arms
In the ward wherein the wounded prisoners lay.

To My Ward-Sister on Night Duty

Through the night-watches of our House of Sighs
    In capable serenity of mind
    You steadily achieve the tasks designed
With calm, half-smiling, interested eyes;
Though all-unknowing, confidently wise
    Concerning pain you never felt, you find
Content from uneventful years arise
    As you toil on, mechanically kind.

So thus far have your smooth days passed, but when
    The tempest none escape shall cloud your sky,
And life grow dark around you, through your pain
You'll learn the meaning of your mercy then
    To those who blessed you as you passed them by,
Nor seek to tread the untroubled road again.

Epitaph on My Days in Hospital

I found in you a holy place apart,
Sublime endurance, God in man revealed,
Where mending broken bodies slowly healed
My broken heart.

The Lament of the Demobilised

'Four years,' some say consolingly,
   'Oh well,
What's that? You're young. And then it must have been
A very fine experience for you!'

And they forget
How others stayed behind and just got on –
Got on the better since we were away.
And we came home and found
They had achieved, and men revered their names,
But never mentioned ours;
And no one talked heroics now, and we
Must just go back and start again once more.
'You threw four years into the melting-pot –
Did you indeed!' these others cry.
   'Oh well,
The more fool you!'
And we're beginning to agree with them.

The Superfluous Woman

Ghosts crying down the vistas of the years,
Recalling words
Whose echoes long have died;
And kind moss grown
Over the sharp and blood-bespattered stones
Which cut our feet upon the ancient ways.

But who will look for my coming?

Long busy days where many meet and part;
Crowded aside
Remembered hours of hope;
And city streets
Grown dark and hot with eager multitudes
Hurrying homeward whither respite waits.

But who will seek me at nightfall?

Light fading where the chimneys cut the sky;
Footsteps that pass,
Nor tarry at my door.
And far away,
Behind the row of crosses, shadows black
Stretch out long arms before the smouldering sun.

But who will give me my children?

Wilfred Owen
1893 – 1918

Wilfred Owen grew up in Birkenhead and Shrewsbury, the son of a railway official. Frustrated in his attempts to win a scholarship to pay for university studies, his first employment was as a lay assistant to the Vicar of Dunsden. Owen had a close relationship with his mother, a devout Evangelical Christian, but he began to lose his own faith and in 1913, partly because of ill health, moved to south-west France to work as a teacher.

He returned to England in 1915 and enlisted with the Artists' Rifles. He was later commissioned into the Manchester Regiment and went to France at the end of December 1916. In May 1917 he was diagnosed as suffering from shell shock. He was sent for treatment to Craiglockhart Hospital, where he met Siegfried Sassoon, who was to have a significant influence on the way he wrote about the war. Owen returned to active service and in September 1918 was back at the front. He showed exceptional courage in the final advance on German lines and was awarded the Military Cross.

Owen was killed one week before the war ended, shot while crossing the Sambre and Oise Canal on a raft. His poems were first published in book form two years later, together with a Preface that he himself had drafted: 'Above all I am not concerned with Poetry. My subject is War, and the pity of War. The Poetry is in the pity.'

Anthem for Doomed Youth

What passing-bells for these who die as cattle?
   – Only the monstrous anger of the guns.
   Only the stuttering rifles' rapid rattle
Can patter out their hasty orisons.
No mockeries now for them; no prayers nor bells;
   Nor any voice of mourning save the choirs, –
The shrill, demented choirs of wailing shells;
   And bugles calling for them from sad shires.

What candles may be held to speed them all?
   Not in the hands of boys but in their eyes
Shall shine the holy glimmers of goodbyes.
   The pallor of girls' brows shall be their pall;
Their flowers the tenderness of patient minds,
And each slow dusk a drawing-down of blinds.

1914

War broke: and now the Winter of the world
With perishing great darkness closes in.
The foul tornado, centred at Berlin,
Is over all the width of Europe whirled,
Rending the sails of progress. Rent or furled
Are all Art's ensigns. Verse wails. Now begin
Famines of thought and feeling. Love's wine's thin.
The grain of human Autumn rots, down-hurled.

For after Spring had bloomed in early Greece,
And Summer blazed her glory out with Rome,
An Autumn softly fell, a harvest home,
A slow grand age, and rich with all increase.
But now, for us, wild Winter, and the need
Of sowings for new Spring, and blood for seed.

Apologia pro Poemate Meo

I, too, saw God through mud, –
    The mud that cracked on cheeks when wretches smiled.
    War brought more glory to their eyes than blood,
    And gave their laughs more glee than shakes a child.

Merry it was to laugh there –
    Where death becomes absurd and life absurder.
    For power was on us as we slashed bones bare
    Not to feel sickness or remorse of murder.

I, too, have dropped off Fear –
    Behind the barrage, dead as my platoon,
    And sailed my spirit surging light and clear
    Past the entanglement where hopes lay strewn;

And witnessed exultation –
    Faces that used to curse me, scowl for scowl,
    Shine and lift up with passion of oblation,
    Seraphic for an hour; though they were foul.

I have made fellowships –
    Untold of happy lovers in old song.
    For love is not the binding of fair lips
    With the soft silk of eyes that look and long,

By Joy, whose ribbon slips, –
    But wound with war's hard wire whose stakes are strong;
    Bound with the bandage of the arm that drips;
    Knit in the webbing of the rifle-thong.

I have perceived much beauty
    In the hoarse oaths that kept our courage straight;
    Heard music in the silentness of duty;
    Found peace where shell-storms spouted reddest spate.

Nevertheless, except you share
    With them in hell the sorrowful dark of hell,
    Whose world is but the trembling of a flare
    And heaven but as the highway for a shell,

You shall not hear their mirth:
    You shall not come to think them well content
    By any jest of mine. These men are worth
    Your tears. You are not worth their merriment.

Dulce et Decorum Est

Bent double, like old beggars under sacks,
Knock-kneed, coughing like hags, we cursed through sludge,
Till on the haunting flares we turned our backs
And towards our distant rest began to trudge.
Men marched asleep. Many had lost their boots
But limped on, blood-shod. All went lame; all blind;
Drunk with fatigue; deaf even to the hoots
Of tired, outstripped Five-Nines that dropped behind.

Gas! GAS! Quick, boys! — An ecstasy of fumbling,
Fitting the clumsy helmets just in time;
But someone still was yelling out and stumbling,
And flound'ring like a man in fire or lime...
Dim, through the misty panes and thick green light,
As under a green sea, I saw him drowning.

In all my dreams, before my helpless sight,
He plunges at me, guttering, choking, drowning.

If in some smothering dreams you too could pace
Behind the wagon that we flung him in,
And watch the white eyes writhing in his face,
His hanging face, like a devil's sick of sin;
If you could hear, at every jolt, the blood
Come gargling from the froth-corrupted lungs,
Obscene as cancer, bitter as the cud
Of vile, incurable sores on innocent tongues, –
My friend, you would not tell with such high zest

To children ardent for some desperate glory,
The old Lie: Dulce et decorum est
Pro patria mori.

Strange Meeting

It seemed that out of battle I escaped
Down some profound dull tunnel, long since scooped
Through granites which titanic wars had groined.

Yet also there encumbered sleepers groaned,
Too fast in thought or death to be bestirred.
Then, as I probed them, one sprang up, and stared
With piteous recognition in fixed eyes,
Lifting distressful hands, as if to bless.
And by his smile, I knew that sullen hall, –
By his dead smile I knew we stood in Hell.

With a thousand pains that vision's face was grained;
Yet no blood reached there from the upper ground,
And no guns thumped, or down the flues made moan.
'Strange friend,' I said, 'here is no cause to mourn.'
'None,' said that other, 'save the undone years,
The hopelessness. Whatever hope is yours,
Was my life also; I went hunting wild
After the wildest beauty in the world,
Which lies not calm in eyes, or braided hair,
But mocks the steady running of the hour,
And if it grieves, grieves richlier than here.
For by my glee might many men have laughed,

And of my weeping something had been left,
Which must die now. I mean the truth untold,
The pity of war, the pity war distilled.
Now men will go content with what we spoiled,
Or, discontent, boil bloody, and be spilled.
They will be swift with swiftness of the tigress.
None will break ranks, though nations trek from progress.
Courage was mine, and I had mystery,
Wisdom was mine, and I had mastery:
To miss the march of this retreating world
Into vain citadels that are not walled.
Then, when much blood had clogged their chariot-wheels,
I would go up and wash them from sweet wells,
Even with truths that lie too deep for taint.
I would have poured my spirit without stint
But not through wounds; not on the cess of war.
Foreheads of men have bled where no wounds were.

'I am the enemy you killed, my friend.
I knew you in this dark: for so you frowned
Yesterday through me as you jabbed and killed.
I parried; but my hands were loath and cold.
Let us sleep now ...'

Futility

Move him into the sun –
Gently its touch awoke him once,
At home, whispering of fields half-sown.
Always it woke him, even in France,

Until this morning and this snow.
If anything might rouse him now
The kind old sun will know.

Think how it wakes the seeds –
Woke once the clays of a cold star.
Are limbs, so dear achieved, are sides
Full-nerved, still warm, too hard to stir?
Was it for this the clay grew tall?
– O what made fatuous sunbeams toil
To break earth's sleep at all?

Mental Cases

Who are these? Why sit they here in twilight?
Wherefore rock they, purgatorial shadows,
Drooping tongues from jaws that slob their relish,
Baring teeth that leer like skulls' teeth wicked?
Stroke on stroke of pain, – but what slow panic,
Gouged these chasms round their fretted sockets?
Ever from their hair and through their hands' palms
Misery swelters. Surely we have perished
Sleeping, and walk hell; but who these hellish?

– These are men whose minds the Dead have ravished.
Memory fingers in their hair of murders,
Multitudinous murders they once witnessed.
Wading sloughs of flesh these helpless wander,
Treading blood from lungs that had loved laughter.
Always they must see these things and hear them,

Batter of guns and shatter of flying muscles,
Carnage incomparable, and human squander
Rucked too thick for these men's extrication.

Therefore still their eyeballs shrink tormented
Back into their brains, because on their sense
Sunlight seems a blood-smear; night comes blood-black;
Dawn breaks open like a wound that bleeds afresh.
– Thus their heads wear this hilarious, hideous,
Awful falseness of set-smiling corpses.
– Thus their hands are plucking at each other;
Picking at the rope-knouts of their scourging;
Snatching after us who smote them, brother,
Pawing us who dealt them war and madness.

The Send-Off

Down the close darkening lanes they sang their way
To the siding-shed,
And lined the train with faces grimly gay.

Their breasts were stuck all white with wreath and spray
As men's are, dead.

Dull porters watched them, and a casual tramp
Stood staring hard,
Sorry to miss them from the upland camp.

Then, unmoved, signals nodded, and a lamp
Winked to the guard.

So secretly, like wrongs hushed-up, they went.
They were not ours:
We never heard to which front these were sent;

Nor there if they yet mock what women meant
Who gave them flowers.

Shall they return to beating of great bells
In wild train-loads?
A few, a few, too few for drums and yells,

May creep back, silent, to village wells,
Up half-known roads.

The Parable of the Old Man and the Young

So Abram rose, and clave the wood, and went,
And took the fire with him, and a knife.
And as they sojourned both of them together,
Isaac the first-born spake and said, My Father,
Behold the preparations, fire and iron,
But where the lamb, for this burnt-offering?
Then Abram bound the youth with belts and straps,
And builded parapets and trenches there,
And stretchèd forth the knife to slay his son.
When lo! an Angel called him out of heaven,
Saying, Lay not thy hand upon the lad,
Neither do anything to him, thy son.
Behold! Caught in a thicket by its horns,
A Ram. Offer the Ram of Pride instead.

But the old man would not so, but slew his son,
And half the seed of Europe, one by one.

Exposure

Our brains ache, in the merciless iced east winds that knive
     us...
Wearied we keep awake because the night is silent...
Low, drooping flares confuse our memory of the salient...
Worried by silence, sentries whisper, curious, nervous,
    But nothing happens.

Watching, we hear the mad gusts tugging on the wire,
Like twitching agonies of men among its brambles.
Northward, incessantly, the flickering gunnery rumbles,
Far off, like a dull rumour of some other war.
    What are we doing here?

The poignant misery of dawn begins to grow...
We only know war lasts, rain soaks, and clouds sag stormy.
Dawn massing in the east her melancholy army
Attacks once more in ranks on shivering ranks of grey,
    But nothing happens.

Sudden successive flights of bullets streak the silence.
Less deathly than the air that shudders black with snow,
With sidelong flowing flakes that flock, pause, and renew;
We watch them wandering up and down the wind's
    nonchalance,
    But nothing happens.

Pale flakes with fingering stealth come feeling for our faces –
We cringe in holes, back on forgotten dreams, and stare,
>snow-dazed
Deep into grassier ditches. So we drowse, sun-dozed,
Littered with blossoms trickling where the blackbird fusses,
>– Is it that we are dying?

Slowly our ghosts drag home: glimpsing the sunk fires,
>glozed
With crusted dark-red jewels; crickets jingle there;
For hours the innocent mice rejoice: the house is theirs;
Shutters and doors, all closed: on us the doors are closed, –
>We turn back to our dying.

Since we believe not otherwise can kind fires burn;
Nor ever suns smile true on child, or field, or fruit.
For God's invincible spring our love is made afraid;
Therefore, not loath, we lie out here; therefore were born,
>For love of God seems dying.

Tonight, this frost will fasten on this mud and us,
Shrivelling many hands, puckering foreheads crisp.
The burying-party, picks and shovels in shaking grasp,
Pause over half-known faces. All their eyes are ice,
>But nothing happens.

The Sentry

We'd found an old Boche dug-out, and he knew,
And gave us hell; for shell on frantic shell
Lit full on top, but never quite burst through.
Rain, guttering down in waterfalls of slime,
Kept slush waist-high and rising hour by hour,
And choked the steps too thick with clay to climb.
What murk of air remained stank old, and sour
With fumes from whizz-bangs, and the smell of men
Who'd lived there years, and left their curse in the den,
If not their corpses...

          There we herded from the blast
Of whizz-bangs; but one found our door at last, –
Buffeting eyes and breath, snuffing the candles,
And thud! flump! thud! down the steep steps came
     thumping
And sploshing in the flood, deluging muck,
The sentry's body; then his rifle, handles
Of old Boche bombs, and mud in ruck on ruck.
We dredged it up, for dead, until he whined,
'O sir – my eyes, – I'm blind, – I'm blind, – I'm blind.'
Coaxing, I held a flame against his lids
And said if he could see the least blurred light
He was not blind; in time they'd get all right.
'I can't,' he sobbed. Eyeballs, huge-bulged like squids',
Watch my dreams still, – yet I forgot him there
In posting Next for duty, and sending a scout
To beg a stretcher somewhere, and flound'ring about
To other posts under the shrieking air.

Those other wretches, how they bled and spewed,
And one who would have drowned himself for good, –
I try not to remember these things now.
Let Dread hark back for one word only: how,
Half-listening to that sentry's moans and jumps,
And the wild chattering of his shivered teeth,
Renewed most horribly whenever crumps
Pummelled the roof and slogged the air beneath, –
Through the dense din, I say, we heard him shout
'I see your lights!' – But ours had long gone out.

Smile, Smile, Smile

Head to limp head, the sunk-eyed wounded scanned
Yesterday's *Mail;* the casualties (typed small)
And (large) Vast Booty from our Latest Haul.
Also, they read of Cheap Homes, not yet planned,
'For', said the paper, 'when this war is done
The men's first instincts will be making homes.
Meanwhile their foremost need is aerodromes,
It being certain war has but begun.
Peace would do wrong to our undying dead, –
The sons we offered might regret they died
If we got nothing lasting in their stead.
We must be solidly indemnified.
Though all be worthy Victory which all bought,
We rulers sitting in this ancient spot
Would wrong our very selves if we forgot
The greatest glory will be theirs who fought,
Who kept this nation in integrity.'
Nation? – The half-limbed readers did not chafe
But smiled at one another curiously
Like secret men who know their secret safe.
(This is the thing they know and never speak,
That England one by one had fled to France,
Not many elsewhere now, save under France.)
Pictures of these broad smiles appear each week,
And people in whose voice real feeling rings
Say: How they smile! They're happy now, poor things.

Laurence Binyon
1869 – 1943

Laurence Binyon was born in Lancaster, studied Classics at Oxford and worked at the British Museum for forty years, latterly as Keeper of Prints and Drawings. By 1914 he had an established reputation as a poet and art historian. 'For the Fallen', written at the very start of the war, was set to music by Edward Elgar in 1917. Its iconic fourth verse is recited at services of Remembrance and was carved (by Eric Gill, in 1921) on the stone entrance of the British Museum, as well as on countless war memorials.

Over-age for active military service, Binyon enlisted in the County of London Regiment (Territorial Force), manning a machine gun in Holland Park and Woolwich as part of the city's defence against air attack. In July 1915 he volunteered with the French Red Cross, serving at the front as an *ambulancier* and medical orderly. His job involved hard, dirty, menial work, as well as assisting the surgeon during operations, and afterwards burning the amputated limbs. He was shocked by 'the misery, the wasting and maiming', and by 'the horrible slaughter', but wrote to a friend: 'one's great longing is to be made use of in some way or other'.

Binyon later lectured British troops on Chinese civilisation as part of the YMCA education programme for soldiers at the front. He wrote a number of ground-breaking books on English, Japanese and Chinese art, as well as much poetry, including a translation of Dante's *Divine Comedy*.

For the Fallen

With proud thanksgiving, a mother for her children,
England mourns for her dead across the sea.
Flesh of her flesh they were, spirit of her spirit,
Fallen in the cause of the free.

Solemn the drums thrill: Death august and royal
Sings sorrow up into immortal spheres.
There is music in the midst of desolation
And a glory that shines upon our tears.

They went with songs to the battle, they were young,
Straight of limb, true of eye, steady and aglow.
They were staunch to the end against odds uncounted,
They fell with their faces to the foe.

They shall grow not old, as we that are left grow old:
Age shall not weary them, nor the years condemn.
At the going down of the sun and in the morning
We will remember them.

They mingle not with their laughing comrades again;
They sit no more at familiar tables of home;
They have no lot in our labour of the day-time;
They sleep beyond England's foam.

But where our desires are and our hopes profound,
Felt as a well-spring that is hidden from sight,
To the innermost heart of their own land they are known
As the stars are known to the Night;

As the stars that shall be bright when we are dust,
Moving in marches upon the heavenly plain,
As the stars that are starry in the time of our darkness,
To the end, to the end, they remain.

Fetching the Wounded

At the road's end glimmer the station lights;
How small beneath the immense hollow of Night's
Lonely and living silence! Air that raced
And tingled on the eyelids as we faced
The long road stretched between the poplars flying
To the dark behind us, shuddering and sighing
With phantom foliage, lapses into hush.
Magical supersession! The loud rush
Swims into quiet: midnight reassumes
Its solitude; there's nothing but great glooms,
Blurred stars; whispering gusts; the hum of wires.
And swerving leftwards upon noiseless tires
We glide over the grass that smells of dew.
A wave of wonder bathes my body through!
For there in the headlamps' gloom-surrounded beam
Tall flowers spring before us, like a dream,
Each luminous little green leaf intimate
And motionless, distinct and delicate
With powdery white bloom fresh upon the stem,
As if that clear beam had created them
Out of the darkness. Never so intense

I felt the pang of beauty's innocence,
Earthly and yet unearthly.

A sudden call!
We leap to ground, and I forget it all.
Each hurries on his errand; lanterns swing;
Dark shapes cross and re-cross the rails; we bring
Stretchers, and pile and number them; and heap
The blankets ready. Then we wait and keep
A listening ear. Nothing comes yet; all's still.
Only soft gusts upon the wires blow shrill
Fitfully, with a gentle spot of rain.
Then, ere one knows it, the long gradual train
Creeps quietly in and slowly stops. No sound
But a few voices' interchange. Around
Is the immense night-stillness, the expanse
Of faint stars over all the wounds of France.

Now stale odour of blood mingles with keen
Pure smell of grass and dew. Now lantern-sheen
Falls on brown faces opening patient eyes
And lips of gentle answers, where each lies
Supine upon his stretcher, black of beard
Or with young cheeks; on caps and tunics smeared
And stained, white bandages round foot or head
Or arm, discoloured here and there with red.
Sons of all corners of wide France; from Lille,
Douay, the land beneath the invader's heel,
Champagne, Touraine, the fisher-villages
Of Brittany, the valleyed Pyrenees,

Blue coasts of the South, old Paris streets. Argonne
Of ever smouldering battle, that anon
Leaps furious, brothered them in arms. They fell
In the trenched forest scarred with reeking shell.
Now strange the sound comes round them in the night
Of English voices. By the wavering light
Quickly we have borne them, one by one, to the air,
And sweating in the dark lift up with care,
Tense-sinewed, each to his place. The cars at last
Complete their burden: slowly, and then fast
We glide away.

           And the dim round of sky,
Infinite and silent, broods unseeingly
Over the shadowy uplands rolling black
Into far woods, and the long road we track
Bordered with apparitions, as we pass,
Of trembling poplars and lamp-whitened grass,
A brief procession flitting like a thought
Through a brain drowsing into slumber; nought
But we awake in the solitude immense!
But hurting the vague dumbness of my sense
Are fancies wandering the night: there steals
Into my heart, like something that one feels
In darkness, the still presence of far homes
Lost in deep country, and in little rooms
The vacant bed. I touch the world of pain
That is so silent. Then I see again
Only those infinitely patient faces
In the lantern beam, beneath the night's vast spaces,

Amid the shadows and the scented dew;
And those illumined flowers, springing anew
In freshness like a smile of secrecy
From the gloom-buried earth, return to me.
The village sleeps; blank walls, and windows barred.
But lights are moving in the hushed courtyard
As we glide up to the open door. The Chief
Gives every man his order, prompt and brief.
We carry up our wounded, one by one.
The first cock crows: the morrow is begun.

excerpt from The Arras Road

The early night falls on the plain
In cloud and desolating rain.
I see no more, but feel around
The ruined earth, the wounded ground.

There in the dark, on either side
The road, are all the brave who died.
I think not on the battles won;
I think on those whose day is done.

Heaped mud, blear pools, old rusted wire,
Cover their youth and young desire.
Near me they sleep, and they to me
Are dearer than their victory.

excerpt from **Wingless Victory**

Victory! Was that proud word once so dear?
Are difficulty, patience, effort hard
As danger's edge, disputing yard by yard
The adversary without and the mind's fear,
Are these our only angels? friends austere
That find our hidden greatness out, and guard
From the weak hour's betrayal faith unmarred!
For look! how we seem fall'n from what we were.

Worms feed upon the bodies of the brave
Who bled for us: but we bewildered see
Viler worms gnaw the things they died to save.
Old clouds of doubt and weariness oppress.
Happy the dead, we cry, not now to be
In the day of this dissolving littleness!

There is Still Splendour

I

O when will life taste clean again? For the air
Is fouled: the world sees, hears; and each day brings
Vile fume that would corrupt eternal things,
Were they corruptible. Harsh trumpets blare
Victory over the defenceless; there
Beauty and compassion, all that loves the light,
Is outcast; thousands in a homeless night
Climb misery's blind paths to the peak, Despair.

Not only martyr'd flesh, but the mind bleeds.
There's nothing left to call inhuman, so
Defaced is man's name by the things men do.
O worse, yet worse, if the world, seeing this,
The hideous spawn of misbegotten creeds,
Grow used, drugged, deadened, and accept the abyss.

II

There is still splendour: the sea tells of it
From far shores, and where murder's made to lurk
In the clean waters; there, men go to work
Simply, upon their daily business, knit
Together in one cause; they think no whit
Of glory; enough that they are men. To those
Who live by terror, calmly they oppose
What wills, dares, and despises to submit.

And the air tells of it: out of the eye's ken
Wings range and soar, a symbol of the free,
In the same cause, outspeeding the swift wind.
Millions of spirits bear them company.
This is the splendour in the souls of men
Which flames against that treason to mankind.

August Afternoon

Thump of a horse's hoof behind the hedge;
Long stripes of shadow, and green flame in the grass
Between them; discrowned, glaucous poppy-pods
On their tall stalks; a rose
With its great thorns blood-red in the slant light;
Round apples swelling on the apple-boughs:–
Over these, over the rich quiet, comes
Out of no-where a 'plane in the high blue
Driving its angry furrow across the sky,
Outstrips the slow clouds, throbs, an urgent roar,
Right overhead, and fiercely vanishes.
  The quiet has become strange. Like from pools
A noiseless water issuing, memories,
Surmises, apprehensions, traceless thoughts,
Glide with brief visions on the mind, drifting
From shadow into shadow; and then a pang
Sudden as when a meteor scars the night:
See where Christ's blood streams in the firmament!
Dead faces of the young, that see nothing...
The unknown wounds, everywhere, everywhere...
  And then from the inner to the outer sense
Returns the sun-warm quiet on the grass,
The poppy charged with sleep, the red, red thorns,
The stamping of the horse behind the hedge,
The strong slow patience of the living earth
And the apple ripening on the apple-tree
Almost as if I felt it in my flesh.

Edmund Blunden
1896 – 1974

Edmund Blunden grew up in Kent, where he developed a deep love for, and knowledge of, the natural world. He described himself as 'a harmless young shepherd in a soldier's coat'.

An officer in the Royal Sussex Regiment, he served for particularly long periods of duty on the Western Front and fought at Ypres and Passchendaele. In 1916 he was awarded the Military Cross for 'great courage and determination when in charge of a carrying party under heavy fire'.

In 1919 he took up his place to study at Oxford, though settling into civilian life proved difficult. The mental scars of his long war experience were slow to heal. His 1928 memoir, *Undertones of War*, is a vivid account of the trenches: 'Men of the next battalion were found in mud up to the armpits, and their fate was not spoken of; those who found them could not get them out. The whole zone was a corpse, and the mud itself mortified.' After the war he held university positions in Oxford, Tokyo and Hong Kong, and in 1966 succeeded Robert Graves as Professor of Poetry at Oxford.

Blunden edited early collections of the work of Wilfred Owen and Ivor Gurney, and wrote about poets who had influenced him, including John Clare and Thomas Hardy. At Oxford he was tutor to Keith Douglas, the most accomplished soldier-poet of the Second World War.

Festubert, 1916

Tired with dull grief, grown old before my day,
I sit in solitude and only hear
Long silent laughters, murmurings of dismay,
The lost intensities of hope and fear;
In those old marshes yet the rifles lie,
On the thin breastwork flutter the grey rags,
The very books I read are there – and I
Dead as the men I loved, wait while life drags

Its wounded length from those sad streets of war
Into green places here, that were my own;
But now what once was mine is mine no more,
I look for such friends here and I find none.
With such strong gentleness and tireless will
Those ruined houses seared themselves in me,
Passionate I look for their dumb story still,
And the charred stub outspeaks the living tree.

I rise up at the singing of a bird
And scarcely knowing slink along the lane,
I dare not give a soul a look or word
For all have homes and none's at home in vain:
Deep red the rose burned in the grim redoubt,
The self-sown wheat around was like a flood,
In the hot path the lizard lolled time out,
The saints in broken shrines were bright as blood.

Sweet Mary's shrine between the sycamores!
There we would go, my friend of friends and I,
And snatch long moments from the grudging wars;
Whose dark made light intense to see them by...
Shrewd bit the morning fog, the whining shots
Spun from the wrangling wire; then in warm swoon
The sun hushed all but the cool orchard plots,
We crept in the tall grass and slept till noon.

Rural Economy (1917)

There was winter in those woods,
And still it was July:
There were Thule solitudes
With thousands huddling nigh;
There the fox had left his den,
The scraped holes hid not stoats but men.

To these woods the rumour teemed
Of peace five miles away;
In sight, hills hovered, houses gleamed
Where last perhaps we lay
Till the cockerels bawled bright morning and
The hours of life slipped the slack hand.

In sight, life's farms sent forth their gear,
Here rakes and ploughs lay still,
Yet, save some curious clods, all here
Was raked and ploughed with a will.
The sower was the ploughman too,
And iron seeds broadcast he threw.

What husbandry could outdo this?
With flesh and blood he fed
The planted iron that nought amiss
Grew thick and swift and red,
And in a night though ne'er so cold
Those acres bristled a hundredfold.

Nay, even the wood as well as field
This ruseful farmer knew
Could be reduced to plough and tilled,
And if he planned, he'd do;
The field and wood, all bone-fed loam,
Shot up a roaring harvest-home.

The Zonnebeke Road

Morning, if this late withered light can claim
Some kindred with that merry flame
Which the young day was wont to fling through space!
Agony stares from each grey face.
And yet the day is come; stand down! stand down!
Your hands unclasp from rifles while you can,
The frost has pierced them to the bended bone!

Why, see old Stevens there, that iron man,
Melting the ice to shave his grotesque chin:
Go ask him, shall we win?
I never liked this bay, some foolish fear
Caught me the first time that I came in here;
That dugout fallen in awakes, perhaps,
Some formless haunting of some corpse's chaps.
True, and wherever we have held the line,
There were such corners, seeming-saturnine
For no good cause.

   Now where Haymarket starts,
That is no place for soldiers with weak hearts;
The minenwerfers have it to the inch.
Look, how the snow-dust whisks along the road,
Piteous and silly; the stones themselves must flinch
In this east wind; the low sky like a load
Hangs over, a dead-weight. But what a pain
Must gnaw where its clay cheek
Crushes the shell chopped trees that fang the plain –
The ice-bound throat gulps out a gargoyle shriek.
The wretched wire before the village line
Rattles like rusty brambles or dead bine,
And then the daylight oozes into dun;
Black pillars, those are trees where roadways run.
Even Ypres now would warm our souls; fond fool,
Our tour's but one night old, seven more to cool!
O screaming dumbness, O dull clashing death,
Shreds of dead grass and willows, homes and men,
Watch as you will, men clench their chattering teeth
And freeze you back with that one hope, disdain.

Concert Party: Busseboom

The stage was set, the house was packed,
  The famous troop began;
Our laughter thundered, act by act;
  Time light as sunbeams ran.

Dance sprang and spun and neared and fled,
  Jest chirped at gayest pitch,
Rhythm dazzled, action sped
  Most comically rich.

With generals and lame privates both
  Such charms worked wonders, till
The show was over – lagging, loth
  We faced the sunset chill;

And standing on the sandy way,
  With the cracked church peering past,
We heard another matinée,
  We heard the maniac blast

Of barrage south by Saint Eloi,
  And the red lights flaming there
Called madness: Come, my bonny boy,
  And dance to the latest air.

To this new concert, white we stood;
  Cold certainty held our breath;
While men in the tunnels below Larch Wood
  Were kicking men to death.

Report on Experience

I have been young, and now am not too old;
And I have seen the righteous forsaken,
His health, his honour and his quality taken.
　　This is not what we were formerly told.

I have seen a green country, useful to the race,
Knocked silly with guns and mines, its villages vanished,
Even the last rat and the last kestrel banished –
　　God bless us all, this was peculiar grace.

I knew Seraphina; Nature gave her hue,
Glance, sympathy, note, like one from Eden.
I saw her smile warp, heard her lyric deaden;
　　She turned to harlotry; – this I took to be new.

Say what you will, our God sees how they run.
These disillusions are His curious proving
That He loves humanity and will go on loving;
　　Over there are faith, life, virtue in the sun.

'Can You Remember?'

Yes, I still remember
The whole thing in a way;
Edge and exactitude
Depend on the day.

Of all that prodigious scene
There seems scanty loss,
Though mists mainly float and screen
Canal, spire and fosse;

Though commonly I fail to name
That once obvious Hill,
And where we went and whence we came
To be killed, or kill.

Those mists are spiritual
And luminous-obscure,
Evolved of countless circumstance
Of which I am sure;

Of which, at the instance
Of sound, smell, change and stir,
New-old shapes for ever
Intensely recur.

And some are sparkling, laughing, singing,
Young, heroic, mild;
And some incurable, twisted,
Shrieking, dumb, defiled.

May Cannan
1893 – 1973

May Wedderburn Cannan grew up in
Oxford, where her father was Dean of
Trinity College. Before the war she
trained in first aid and nursing, serving
with a local branch of the Voluntary
Aid Detachment (VAD). In 1915 she volunteered to run the
canteen at the Rouen railhead, serving soldiers travelling to
and from the front line: 'When the whistle blew they stood
to save the King and the roof came off the sheds, 2,000 men,
maybe, singing – it was the most moving thing I knew. Then
there'd be the thunder of seats pushed back, the stamp of
army boots on the pave, and as the train went out they sang
"Tipperary".'

In 1918 she joined the Espionage Section of the British
Mission in Paris. Her fiancé, Major Bevil Quiller-Couch,
survived some of the worst fighting of the war, but died in the
flu pandemic of 1919. Her poems about the war were written,
she said, 'for those who were still convinced of the right of the
cause for which they had taken up arms'. One reader, PJ Slater
of the Royal Flying Corps, wrote to her asking to meet, and
they later married.

Cannan worked in various roles for the Oxford University
Press, King's College, London and the library at the
Athenaeum Club. She stopped writing after Slater's negative
reaction to her novel, *The Lonely Generation* (1934), which
drew on her love affair with Quiller-Couch.

Rouen

April 26 – May 25, 1915

Early morning over Rouen, hopeful, high, courageous
    morning,
And the laughter of adventure and the steepness of the stair,
And the dawn across the river, and the wind across the
    bridges,
And the empty littered station and the tired people there.

Can you recall those mornings and the hurry of awakening,
And the long-forgotten wonder if we should miss the way,
And the unfamiliar faces, and the coming of provisions,
And the freshness and the glory of the labour of the day?

Hot noontide over Rouen, and the sun upon the city,
Sun and dust unceasing, and the glare of cloudless skies,
And the voices of the Indians and the endless stream of
    soldiers,
And the clicking of the tatties, and the buzzing of the flies.

Can you recall those noontides and the reek of steam and
    coffee,
Heavy-laden noontides with the evening's peace to win,
And the little piles of woodbines, and the sticky soda bottles,
And the crushes in the 'Parlour', and the letters coming in?

Quiet night-time over Rouen, and the station full of soldiers,
All the youth and pride of England from the ends of all the
    earth;
And the rifles piled together, and the creaking of the sword-
    belts,

And the faces bent above them, and the gay, heart-breaking
    mirth.

Can I forget the passage from the cool white-bedded Aid
    Post
Past the long sun-blistered coaches of the khaki Red Cross
    train
To the truck train full of wounded, and the weariness and
    laughter,
And 'Good-bye, and thank you, Sister', and the empty yards
    again?

Can you recall the parcels that we made them for the
    railroad,
Crammed and bulging parcels held together by their string,
And the voices of the sergeants who called the Drafts
    together,
And the agony and splendour when they stood to save the
    King?

Can you forget their passing, the cheering and the waving,
The little group of people at the doorway of the shed,
The sudden awful silence when the last train swung to
    darkness,
And the lonely desolation, and the mocking stars o'erhead?

Can you recall the midnights, and the footsteps of night
    watchers,
Men who came from darkness and went back to dark again,
And the shadows on the rail-lines and the all-inglorious
    labour,

And the promise of the daylight firing blue the window-
     pane?

Can you recall the passing through the kitchen door to
     morning,
Morning very still and solemn breaking slowly on the town,
And the early coastways engines that had met the ships at
     daybreak,
And the Drafts just out from England, and the day shift
     coming down?

Can you forget returning slowly, stumbling on the cobbles,
And the white-decked Red Cross barges dropping seawards
     for the tide,
And the search for English papers, and the blessed cool of
     water,
And the peace of half-closed shutters that shut out the
     world outside?

Can I forget the evenings and the sunsets on the island,
And the tall black ships at anchor far below our balcony,
And the distant call of bugles, and the white wine in the
     glasses,
And the long line of the street lamps, stretching Eastwards
     to the sea?

...When the world slips slow to darkness, when the office
     fire burns lower,
My heart goes out to Rouen, Rouen all the world away;
When other men remember I remember our Adventure
And the trains that go from Rouen at the ending of the day.

Lamplight

We planned to shake the world together, you and I
Being young, and very wise;
Now in the light of the green shaded lamp
Almost I see your eyes
Light with the old gay laughter; you and I
Dreamed greatly of an Empire in those days,
Setting our feet upon laborious ways,
And all you asked of fame
Was crossed swords in the Army List,
My Dear, against your name.

We planned a great Empire together, you and I,
Bound only by the sea;
Now in the quiet of a chill Winter's night
Your voice comes hushed to me
Full of forgotten memories: you and I
Dreamed great dreams of our future in those days,
Setting our feet on undiscovered ways,
And all I asked of fame
A scarlet cross on my breast, my Dear,
For the swords by your name.

We shall never shake the world together, you and I,
For you gave your life away;
And I think my heart was broken by the war,
Since on a summer day
You took the road we never spoke of: you and I
Dreamed greatly of an Empire in those days;
You set your feet upon the Western ways

And have no need of fame –
There's a scarlet cross on my breast, my Dear,
And a torn cross with your name.

Paris, November 11, 1918

Down on the boulevards the crowds went by,
The shouting and the singing died away,
And in the quiet we rose to drink the toasts,
Our hearts uplifted to the hour, the Day:
The King – the Army – Navy – the Allies –
England – and Victory. –
And then you turned to me and with low voice
(The tables were abuzz with revelry),
'I have a toast for you and me', you said,
And whispered 'Absent', and we drank
Our unforgotten Dead.
> But I saw Love go lonely down the years,
> And when I drank, the wine was salt with tears.

Paris Leave

Do you remember, in Paris, how we two dined
On your Leave's last night,
And the happy people around us who laughed and sang,
And the great blaze of light.

And the big bow-window over the boulevard
Where our table stood,
And the old French waitress who patted your shoulder and
Told us that love was good.

(We had lingered so long watching the crowds that moved
In the street below,
And saying the swift dear things of Lovers newly met,
That she had guessed us so.)

I remember her smile, and the ring of your spurs
On the polished stair;
And the touch of your hand, and the clear November night,
And the flags everywhere.

I remember the Concorde, and the fountains' splash,
The black captured guns;
And the grey-haired men with their wives who wept and
    kissed, and
The lovers of their sons.

And the French girls with their poilus who linked their
    hands
To dance round us two,
And sang '*Ne passeront pas*', till one broke loose and flung
Her arms wide and kissed you.

She was all France that night, and you brave Angleterre,
The unfailing friend;
And I cried, 'Vive la France', and we told each other again
The War was at an end.

It was so hard to believe it was really won,
And the waiting past;
That the years wherein we knew death were under our feet,
And our Love crowned at last...

I remember most now the faces of the girls,
And the still, clear stars.
We said we were glad later lovers would never know
The bitterness of wars.

The lamp of the courtyard gate was bright on the old
Ribbons on your breast;
And the songs and the voices died down the boulevards.
You said that Love was best.

Ivor Gurney

1890 – 1937

Ivor Gurney grew up in Gloucester and was a boy chorister at the Cathedral. In 1911 he won a composition scholarship to the Royal College of Music. Initially rejected by the Army because of poor eyesight, Gurney enlisted in early 1915 and served as a private in the Gloucestershire Regiment.

He described his life in the ranks in a letter to his friend, Marion Scott: 'The Army is an awful life for an artist […] Either it is slogging along uselessly with a pack or doing nothing but hang about after – or boredom or hell in the trenches. Very little between.' Despite this, he managed to write songs and poems at the front, often contrasting the immediate horror of trench life with memories of a beloved English countryside: 'I cling to life by deliberately trying to lose myself in my thoughts of other things.' He suffered a bullet wound in the spring of 1917, and was gassed later that year at Passchendaele.

Gurney returned to the Royal College after the wa time to study under Ralph Vaughan Williams, but he w restless to concentrate or lead a structured life. He con to be a prolific composer and poet, despite recurrent bc severe mental illness, thought to be part of an underlyin condition, rather than necessarily a result of the war. I he was committed to an asylum for the rest of his life.

Song ('Severn Meadows')

Only the wanderer
    Knows England's graces,
Or can anew see clear
    Familiar faces.

And who loves joy as he
    That dwells in shadows?
Do not forget me quite,
    O Severn meadows.

To His Love

He's gone, and all our plans
    Are useless indeed.
We'll walk no more on Cotswold
    Where the sheep feed
    Quietly and take no heed.

His body that was so quick
    Is not as you
Knew it, on Severn river
    Under the blue
    Driving our small boat through.

You would not know him now...
    But still he died
Nobly, so cover him over
    With violets of pride
    Purple from Severn side.

Cover him, cover him soon!
       And with thick-set
Masses of memoried flowers –
       Hide that red wet
       Thing I must somehow forget.

De Profundis

If only this fear would leave me I could dream of Crickley
    Hill
   And a hundred thousand thoughts of home would visit
     my heart in sleep;
But here the peace is shattered all day by the devil's will,
   And the guns bark night-long to spoil the velvet silence
     deep.

O who could think that once we drank in quiet inns and
    cool
   And saw brown oxen trooping the dry sands to slake
Their thirst at the river flowing, or plunged in a silver pool
   To shake the sleepy drowse off before well awake?

We are stale here, we are covered body and soul and mind
   With mire of the trenches, close clinging and foul,
We have left our old inheritance, our Paradise behind,
   And clarity is lost to us and cleanness of soul.

O blow here, you dusk-airs and breaths of half-light,
    And comfort despairs of your darlings that long
Night and day for sound of your bells, or a sight
    Of your tree-bordered lanes, land of blossom and song.

Autumn will be here soon, but the road of coloured leaves
    Is not for us, the up and down highway where go
Earth's pilgrims to wonder where Malvern upheaves
    That blue-emerald splendour under great clouds of snow.

Some day we'll fill in trenches, level the land and turn
    Once more joyful faces to the country where trees
Bear thickly for good drink, where strong sunsets burn
    Huge bonfires of glory – O God, send us peace!

Hard it is for men of moors or fens to endure
    Exile and hardship, or the northland grey-drear;
But we of the rich plain of sweet airs and pure,
    Oh! Death would take so much from us, how should we
        not fear?

La Gorgue

The long night, the short sleep, and La Gorgue to wander,
So be the Fates were kind and our Commander;
With a mill, and still canal, and like-Stroudway bridges.
One looks back on these as Time's truest riches
Which were so short an escape, so perilous a joy
Since fatigues, weather, Line trouble or any whimsical ploy
Division might hatch out would have finished peace.

There was a house there, (I tell the noted thing)
The kindest woman kept, and an unending string
Of privates as wasps to sugar went in and out.
Friendliness sanctified all there without doubt,
As lovely as the mill above the still green
Canal where the dark fishes went almost unseen.
B Company had come down from Tilleloy
Lousy, thirsty, avid of any employ
Of peace; and this woman in leanest times had plotted
A miracle to amaze the army-witted.
And this was Café-au-lait as princes know it,
And fasting, and poor-struck; dead but not to show it.
A drink of edicts, dooms, a height of tales.
Heat, cream, coffee; the maker tries and fails,
The poet too, where such thirst such mate had.
A campaign thing that makes remembrance sad.

There was light there, too, in the clear North French way.
It blessed the room, and bread, and the mistress giver,
The husband for his wife's sake, and both for a day
Were blessed by many soldiers tired however:
A mark in Time, a Peace, a Making-delay.

Strange Hells

There are strange Hells within the minds War made
Not so often, not so humiliatingly afraid
As one would have expected – the racket and fear guns
     made.
One Hell the Gloucester soldiers they quite put out:
Their first bombardment, when in combined black shout
Of fury, guns aligned, they ducked lower their heads –
And sang with diaphragms fixed beyond all dreads,
That tin and stretched-wire tinkle, that blither of tune:
'Après la guerre fini', till Hell all had come down.
Twelve-inch, six-inch, and eighteen pounders hammering
     Hell's thunders.

Where are they now, on State-doles, or showing shop-
     patterns
Or walking town to town sore in borrowed tatterns
Or begged. Some civic routine one never learns.
The heart burns – but has to keep out of face how heart
     burns.

First Time In

After the dread tales and red yarns of the Line
Anything might have come to us; but the divine
Afterglow brought us up to a Welsh colony
Hiding in sandbag ditches, whispering consolatory
Soft foreign things. Then we were taken in
To low huts candle-lit, shaded close by slitten
Oilsheets, and there but boys gave us kind welcome,
So that we looked out as from the edge of home.
Sang us Welsh things, and changed all former notions
To human hopeful things. And the next day's guns
Nor any Line-pangs ever quite could blot out
That strangely beautiful entry to War's rout;
Candles they gave us, precious and shared over-rations –
Ulysses found little more in his wanderings without doubt.
'David of the White Rock', the 'Slumber Song' so soft, and
        that
Beautiful tune to which roguish words by Welsh pit boys
Are sung – but never more beautiful than here under the
        guns' noise.

IVOR GURNEY

Behind the Line

I suppose France this morning is as white as here
High white clouds veiling the sun, and the mere
Cabbage fields and potato plants lovely to see,
Back behind at Robecq there with the day free.

In the estaminets I suppose the air as cool, and the floor
Grateful dark red; the beer and the different store
Of citron, grenadine, red wine as surely delectable
As in Nineteen Sixteen; with the round stains on the dark
    table.

Journals Français tell the same news and the queer
Black printed columns give news, but no longer the fear
Of shrapnel or any evil metal torments.
High white morning as here one is sure is on France.

The Bohemians

Certain people would not clean their buttons,
Nor polish buckles after latest fashions,
Preferred their hair long, putties comfortable,
Barely escaping hanging, indeed hardly able;
In Bridge and smoking without army cautions
Spending hours that sped like evil for quickness,
(While others burnished brasses, earned promotions).
These were those ones who jested in the trench,
While others argued of army ways, and wrenched
What little soul they had still further from shape,
And died off one by one, or became officers.

Without the first of dream, the ghost of notions
Of ever becoming soldiers, or smart and neat,
Surprised as ever to find the army capable
Of sounding 'Lights out' to break a game of Bridge,
As to fear candles would set a barn alight:
In Artois or Picardy they lie – free of useless fashions.

The Silent One

Who died on the wires, and hung there, one of two –
Who for his hours of life had chattered through
Infinite lovely chatter of Bucks accent;
Yet faced unbroken wires; stepped over, and went,
A noble fool, faithful to his stripes – and ended.
But I weak, hungry, and willing only for the chance
Of line – to fight in the line, lay down under unbroken
Wires, and saw the flashes, and kept unshaken.
Till the politest voice – a finicking accent, said:
'Do you think you might crawl through, there: there's a
        hole?' In the afraid
Darkness, shot at; I smiled, as politely replied –
'I'm afraid not, Sir.' There was no hole no way to be seen.
Nothing but chance of death, after tearing of clothes.
Kept flat, and watched the darkness, hearing bullets
        whizzing –
And thought of music – and swore deep heart's deep oaths.
(Polite to God) – and retreated and came on again.
Again retreated – and a second time faced the screen.

The Mangel-Bury

It was after war; Edward Thomas had fallen at Arras –
I was walking by Gloucester musing on such things
As fill his verse with goodness; it was February; the long
    house
Straw-thatched of the mangels stretched two wide wings;
And looked as part of the earth heaped up by dead soldiers
In the most fitting place – along the hedge's yet-bare lines.
West-spring breathed there early, that none foreign divines.
Across the flat country the rattling of the cart sounded:
Heavy of wood, jingling of iron; as he neared me I waited
For the chance perhaps of heaving at those great rounded
Ruddy or orange things – and right to be rolled and hefted
By a body like mine, soldier still, and clean from water.
Silent he assented; till the cart was drifted
High with those creatures, so right in size and matter.
We threw with our bodies swinging; blood in my ears
    singing;
His was the thick-set sort of farmer, but well built –
Perhaps long before his blood's name ruled all:
Watched all things for his own. If my luck had so willed
Many questions of lordship I had heard him tell – old
Names, rumours. But my pain to more moving called
And him to some barn business far in the fifteen acre field.

It is Near Toussaints

It is near Toussaints, the living and dead will say:
'Have they ended it? What has happened to Gurney?'
And along the leaf-strewn roads of France many brown
    shades
Will go, recalling singing, and a comrade for whom also they
Had hoped well. His honour them had happier made.
Curse all that hates good. When I spoke of my breaking
(Not understood) in London, they imagined of the taking
Vengeance, and seeing things were different in future.
(A musician was a cheap, honourable and nice creature.)
Kept sympathetic silence; heard their packs creaking
And burst into song – Hilaire Belloc was all our Master.
On the night of all the dead, they will remember me,
Pray Michael, Nicholas, Maries lost in Novembery
River-mist in the old City of our dear love, and batter
At doors about the farms crying 'Our war poet is lost',
'Madame – no bon!' – and cry his two names, warningly,
    sombrely.

War Books

What did they expect of our toil and extreme
Hunger – the perfect drawing of a heart's dream?
Did they look for a book of wrought art's perfection,
Who promised no reading, nor praise, nor publication?
Out of the heart's sickness the spirit wrote.
For delight, or to escape hunger, or of war's worst anger,
When the guns died to silence, and men would gather sense
Somehow together, and find this was life indeed.
And praise another's nobleness, or to Cotswold get hence.
There we wrote – Corbie Ridge – or in Gonnehem at rest.
Or Fauquissart or world's death songs, ever the best.
One made sorrows' praise passing the church where silence
Opened for the long quivering strokes of the bell –
Another wrote all soldiers' praise, and of France and night's
    stars –
Served his guns, got immortality, and died well.
But Ypres played another trick with its danger on me,
Kept still the needing and loving-of-action body;
Gave no candles, and nearly killed me twice as well.
And no souvenirs, though I risked my life in the stuck
    Tanks.
Yet there was praise of Ypres, love came sweet in hospital –
And old Flanders went under to long ages of plough
    thought in my pages.

Bibliography and text sources

Rupert Brooke, *The Complete Poems* (Sidgwick and Jackson, 1935)

Charles Hamilton Sorley, *Collected Poems* ed. Jean Moorcroft Wilson
   (Cecil Woolf, 1985)

Robert Graves, *Complete Poems* ed. Beryl Graves and Dunstan Ward
   (Carcanet Press Limited, 2000)

Siegfried Sassoon, *Collected Poems 1908–1956* (Faber, 1961)

Mary Borden, 'The Song of the Mud' and 'Unidentified', from *The Forbidden Zone*
   (Heinemann, 1929); 'No, no!' and 'See how the withered leaves' texts are taken
   directly from manuscripts in the Spears Papers at the Churchill Archives Centre,
   Churchill College, Cambridge; 'Come to me quickly' text is taken from the
   manuscript in the Mary Borden Collection, Howard Gotlieb Archival Research
   Center at Boston University. 'No, no!' and 'See how the withered leaves'
   were published in *War Literature and the Arts: An International Journal of the
   Humanities*, vol. 23, 2011 by Dr. Marcia Phillips McGowan. 'Come to me quickly'
   was published in *Modernism/Modernity*, John Hopkins University Press, September
   2009, vol. 16 number 3.

Geoffrey Studdert Kennedy, *The Unutterable Beauty: The Collected Poetry of
   GA Studdert Kennedy* (Hodder & Stoughton, 1927)

Edward Thomas, *Collected Poems* ed. Edna Longley (Bloodaxe, 2008)

David Jones, *In Parenthesis* (Faber, 1937)

Isaac Rosenberg, *Isaac Rosenberg* ed. Vivien Noakes (Oxford University Press, 2008)

Vera Brittain, *Poems from the War and After* (Macmillan, 1937)

Wilfred Owen, *The War Poems*, ed. Jon Stallworthy (Chatto & Windus, 1984)

Laurence Binyon, *Collected Poems: Lyrical Poems* (Macmillan, 1931);
   The North Star (Macmillan, 1941)

Edmund Blunden, *Selected Poems* ed. Robyn Marsack (Carcanet Press Limited, 1982);
   Undertones of War (Penguin, 1937)

May Wedderburn Cannan, *In War Time* (Blackwell, 1917); *The Splendid Days*
   (Blackwell, 1919)

Ivor Gurney, *Collected Poems* ed. PJ Kavanagh (Carcanet Press Limited, 2004)

Acknowledgements

My thanks for help with the Mary Borden manuscripts to Katharine Thomson, Churchill Archives Centre, Churchill College, Cambridge, as well as to Sean Noel and Jennifer Pino at the Howard Gotlieb Archival Research Center at Boston University, and to Dr Marcia McGowan. I am extremely grateful for the support of Elizabeth Bowers, Madeleine James, Tony Richards, Rebecca Stephens, Matthew Brosnan, Abigail Lelliott and the staff of Imperial War Museums. Thanks are also due to Kay Walters, Librarian at the Athenaeum, Vanessa Davis, Karen MacNaughton, Pilar O'Prey and John Simpson, for their help and advice.

Rupert Brooke – Image © IWM (Q 71073)

Charles Sorley – Image reproduced by kind permission of Taff Gillingham and the Suffolk Regiment

Robert Graves – Carcanet Press Limited for ten poems from *Complete Poems* by Robert Graves, ed. Beryl Graves and Dunstan Ward, Carcanet Press Limited, 2000. Image courtesy of The Robert Graves Estate.

Siegfried Sassoon – Poems copyright Siegfried Sassoon by kind permission of the Estate of George Sassoon. Image © IWM (Q 101780)

Mary Borden – 'No, no!' and 'See how the withered leaves' from the Spears Papers at the Churchill Archives Centre, Churchill College, Cambridge, 'Come to me quickly' from the Mary Borden Collection, Howard Gotlieb Archival Research Center at Boston University, all poems and image reproduced by kind permission of Patrick Aylmer, © Patrick Aylmer.

Geoffrey Studdert Kennedy – Image © Lebrecht Authors

Edward Thomas – Image © IWM (Q 71059)

David Jones – Poems and image reproduced by kind permission of the Trustees of the Estate of David Jones

Isaac Rosenberg – Image reproduced with permission from the Isaac Rosenberg Estate © IWM (HU 59123)

Vera Brittain – Poems are reproduced by permission of Mark Bostridge and T J Brittain-Catlin, Literary Executors of the Vera Brittain Estate, 1970. Image reproduced by permission of The William Ready Division of Archives and Research Collections, McMaster University Library, Ontario.

Wilfred Owen – Image © IWM (Q 101783)

Laurence Binyon – Image © Getty images

Edmund Blunden – Carcanet Press Limited for six poems from *Selected Poems* by Edmund Blunden, ed. Robyn Marsack, Carcanet Press Limited, 1982. David Higham Associates, on behalf of the Edmund Blunden Estate, for image and short extract from *The Undertones of War* by Edmund Blunden published by Penguin.

May Cannan – Poems and image reproduced by permission of Mrs C M Abrahams on behalf of the May Wedderburn Cannan Estate.

Ivor Gurney – Image © The Ivor Gurney Estate